W9-CHL-786

PUTTING
Speed & Accuracy

GAME IMPROVEMENT LIBRARY™

CREDITS

PUTTING
SPEED & ACCURACY

Printed in 2006.

Tom Carpenter
Creative Director

Julie Cisler
Book Design & Production

Michele Teigen
Senior Book Development Coordinator

Steve Hosid
Instruction Editor/Photographer

Steve Ellis
Editor

Ward Clayton   **Leo McCullagh**
Bob Combs   **Mike Mueller**
PGA TOUR

Cover Image © 2001 Stan Badz/PGA TOUR

Special thanks to the following golf courses for allowing us to shoot on location:
TPC at Sawgrass: Ponte Vedra Beach, Florida
Arnold Palmer's Bay Hill Club & Lodge: Orlando, Florida
PGA of Southern California Golf Club: Calimesa, California
TPC at The Canyons: The Resort at Summerlin, Las Vegas, Nevada
Tanglewood Park: Clemmons, North Carolina

Acknowledgements
"To the members of the PGA TOUR Partners Club I meet at tournaments around the country: Your questions, comments and support help create articles and books that truly reflect the needs of our outstanding membership."
—*Steve Hosid*

© 2001 PGA TOUR Partners Club
4 5 6 7 8 / 08 07 06 05
ISBN 1-58159-132-2

PGA TOUR Partners Club
12301 Whitewater Drive
Minnetonka, Minnesota 55343
www.partnersclubonline.com

ABOUT THE AUTHOR/ PHOTOGRAPHER

Steve Hosid is instruction editor, contributing writer and photographer for *PGA TOUR Partners* magazine and the Club's Game Improvement Library. He is co-author of *The Complete Idiot's Guide to Healthy Stretching* (with Chris Verna), and *Golf for Everybody* (with Brad Brewer, former director of The Arnold Palmer Golf Academies), and has collaborated on books with LPGA star Michelle McGann and tennis player MaliVai Washington.

Steve is a graduate of the University of Southern California. He and his wife, Jill, live with two non-golfing Borzoi Wolfhounds on the 13th hole at Arnold Palmer's Bay Hill Club & Lodge in Orlando, Florida.

Steve Hosid with just a "few" choices from the enormous selection of available putters. His favorite? Whichever one is working!

CONTENTS

INTRODUCTION

"Putt like a kid" was the simple advice my friend Brad Faxon gave our Partners Club readers in an instruction article a few years back. He was right. As with so many successful solutions to complicated problems, a simple approach sometimes provides the best remedy.

As a kid my only thought was to hole the putt, regardless if it was a 30-footer or a three-footer. When I practiced with my friends we competed to see how many putts in a row we could make from a given distance. Little thought was given to mechanics. We just looked at the hole and went for it.

That same *feeling* (which is a word you will see over and over again in this book) comes back to me when I first come out of the locker room, open a fresh sleeve of balls and practice putting while casually talking to some friends. Because I'm relaxed and just looking at the hole, with my mind at ease, it's amazing how good a putter I can be.

successful. While their individual styles may not suit you, much can be learned from their advice, drills and practice lessons.

My admiration for Martin Hall grows with each project we work on. Long respected as one of the game's finest teachers, he makes practicing fun. The reason I no longer concern myself with mechanics during a round is because they have become second nature as a result of Martin's drills.

Professional golfers are competitive even while practicing. They invent games to keep their interest level high during long practice sessions. In this book, Jim Furyk will show you the game played by the "Ponte Vedra Boys" on the practice green at The TPC at Sawgrass. The "boys" include Furyk and TOUR pals David Duval, Rocco Mediate, Fred Funk and Frank Lickliter.

You'll discover that choosing the correct putter is as important as having good mechanics. You'll also find loads of information on selecting a putter, and visit with the folks who design them.

But I confess: Once out on the course, my thoughts became overly concerned with mechanics. That changed while collaborating on this book with our four PGA TOUR experts and noted instructor Martin Hall. Now when I putt all my thoughts are about feeling the speed and holing the putt. I still work on my mechanics—just not when I play.

Your putting style can't be forced. There's no one technique that fits all. The important thing is to find a style with which *you* are comfortable. Each of our professionals has a different technique and, in some cases, a different length putter. All are

While some books deal with theories, this book offers advice only a PGA TOUR player can share. The time has come for permanent putting improvement.

-Steve Hosid-

MEET THE PLAYERS

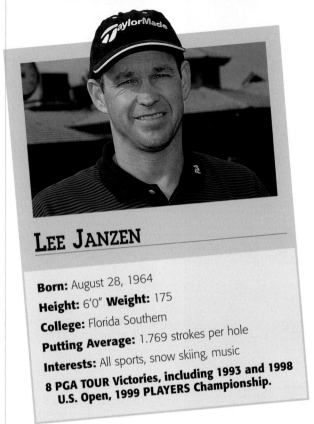

LEE JANZEN

Born: August 28, 1964

Height: 6'0" **Weight:** 175

College: Florida Southern

Putting Average: 1.769 strokes per hole

Interests: All sports, snow skiing, music

8 PGA TOUR Victories, including 1993 and 1998 U.S. Open, 1999 PLAYERS Championship.

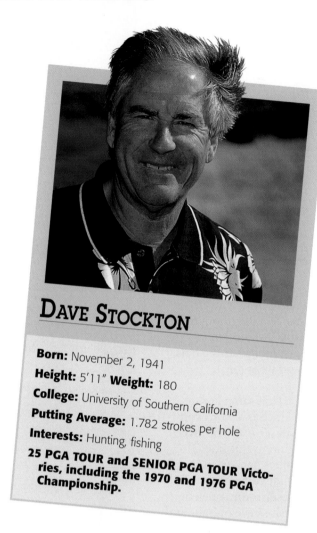

DAVE STOCKTON

Born: November 2, 1941

Height: 5'11" **Weight:** 180

College: University of Southern California

Putting Average: 1.782 strokes per hole

Interests: Hunting, fishing

25 PGA TOUR and SENIOR PGA TOUR Victories, including the 1970 and 1976 PGA Championship.

Like a lot of guys on the PGA TOUR, I grew up playing other sports before taking up golf. My favorite sport was baseball, but the season ended midway through the school year, leaving my summers open. Some of my buddies played golf, so I took it up and here I am.

Winning two U.S. Open Championships is a dream come true. The first time I saw the Open on television, Jack Nicklaus won at Baltusrol Golf Club. My first Open title in 1993 was on the same course after a great battle with my friend Payne Stewart. We dueled again at The Olympic Club in San Francisco in 1998 when I won my second Open.

Becoming a good putter affects the way you play the game. Putting well during a round, and making all the short putts, allows you to be more aggressive with your approach shots. Even if you miss the green, you know you can make a par with a good chip.

Conversely, putting poorly forces you to play more conservatively. Instead of firing at the pins, you aim for the center of the green. The result is longer birdie putts, which you are less likely to make.

—Lee Janzen

I grew up on a golf course in California. At age 5 I was challenging people to putting contests. Growing up in California also meant surfing. Unfortunately, a surfing accident broke my back, and the lingering effect is that a long putting practice session for me is limited to only 15 minutes.

While the injury shortened my practice time, it didn't affect my putting skills. Why? Because I believe putting centers on visualization and reading greens, not on mechanics. Putting is very mental, and staying positive is the key to reducing your putting strokes.

There are two words I want you to avoid when discussing putting. The first is "hit," as in "hit the putt." You don't "hit a putt," you "roll a putt." The next word is "try." If you "try" to make a putt, chances are you will miss. Be positive and become a better putter!

—Dave Stockton

JIM FURYK

Born: May 12, 1970

Height: 6'2" **Weight:** 200

College: University of Arizona

Putting Average: 1.764 strokes per hole

Interests: All sports, fishing, Pittsburgh Steelers and Jacksonville Jaguars

6 PGA TOUR Victories, including 3 times at the Las Vegas Invitational. Member of victorious 1999 U.S. Ryder Cup Team.

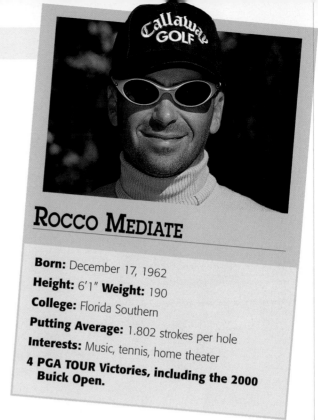

ROCCO MEDIATE

Born: December 17, 1962

Height: 6'1" **Weight:** 190

College: Florida Southern

Putting Average: 1.802 strokes per hole

Interests: Music, tennis, home theater

4 PGA TOUR Victories, including the 2000 Buick Open.

My dad is a golf professional and taught me the sport when I was 12. My cross-handed putting grip stems from a conversation my dad had with Arnold Palmer and Gary Player during a Pennsylvania golf outing.

He asked each of these legends, "If you could change one thing about your game, what would it be?" They both said they would start putting cross-handed.

Having never putted with a conventional grip, it's hard for me to compare the two techniques. Putting is such an individualistic part of the game. My suggestion is to experiment and develop a style that is both comfortable and works.

I putt cross-handed on every stroke, but SENIOR PGA TOUR player Larry Nelson switches sometimes in mid-round to a cross-handed style to rekindle his feel. Even if you don't choose to putt cross-handed, I'll share some information and insight that I hope will make you a better putter.

—Jim Furyk

In 1990, while playing with Jim Ferree, I putted so poorly that I reluctantly agreed to try a long putter for the first time. Jim, who used one, insisted I try it. Guess what? It worked! I've also been fortunate to have a great amateur player and longtime friend of mine, Randy Sonnier of Kingston, Texas, help me with my putting.

Long putters put less stress on your back than conventional putters do. My bad back can't stand up to the rigors of lengthy practice sessions with the shorter, conventional putters. Now I can stand tall while practicing, which is a huge bonus because, believe me, if you don't practice putting you won't be on the PGA TOUR for long.

I'll show you how to hole more putts by improving your speed and accuracy. During a round TOUR players think mostly about speed while amateurs are more concerned about line and mechanics.

—Rocco Mediate

MARTIN HALL

Martin Hall, one of the game's top instructors, provides his proven practice drills throughout this book. Hall appears regularly on the PGA TOUR Partners Video Series and has been selected as one of the 50 best golf instructors in the U.S.

1

ASK THE PROS

"I played like Doug Sanders and putted like Colonel Sanders."—*Chi Chi Rodriguez*

Before beginning the instruction phase of putting—and the process of turning you into a better putter—we gathered our four PGA TOUR professionals together for a question and answer session. Lee Janzen, Dave Stockton, Jim Furyk and Rocco Mediate share their thoughts and provide a TOUR player's insight into this critical phase of the game.

Lee discusses why he believes putting techniques have changed over the years and explains why a blended stroke works better today. Dave reveals that his "interim target" aiming point is less than an inch from the ball, and Rocco introduces the idea of using the toe of the putter when the ball rests against the collar. Jim discusses the plumb bob technique.

Each of the questions and answers refers you to the chapter that covers that specific topic. Your transformation into a better putter is about to begin.

"When putting, it's better to have a positive thought, even if it's the wrong one, than confuse yourself and not be sure at all."—*Dave Stockton*

PRO:
LEE JANZEN

QUESTION: WHY HAVE PUTTING STYLES CHANGED SO MUCH OVER THE YEARS?

ANSWER:

Replays of old tournaments show players with wristy strokes because the greens were slower then. This technique helped players lift the ball off the surface to start it rolling.

Today's TOUR players use their shoulders more in the stroke. Big shoulder muscles have less room for error and provide more stability for short putts. However, I think it's hard to make 20- or 30-foot putts using only your shoulders. You also need your hands for feel.

The key to putting success is keeping the putter head close to the ground *throughout* the stroke. My stroke is a blend of using my shoulders and hands. In Chapter 2 you can take a closer look at all our strokes.

— LEE

PRO:
DAVE STOCKTON

QUESTION: DO YOU GIVE MORE CONSIDERATION TO LINE OR SPEED WHEN READING A PUTT?

ANSWER:

The distance you roll a putt is more important than the line. By distance I mean the correct speed. I was taught to never leave a putt short but also not to knock it more than 18 inches past the hole.

With this approach to speed, I want the ball to die into the hole. Even a miss should leave me a putt of no more than a foot-and-a-half. In Chapter 5 we'll help you learn the basics for the pace and speed you need to sink both long and short putts.

Terrain changes also play a pivitol role in determining speed. We show you how to read the greens like a pro in Chapter 4.

— DAVE

PRO: JIM FURYK

QUESTIONS: YOU PUTT CROSS-HANDED AND ROCCO PUTTS WITH A LONG PUTTER. WHAT IS THE BEST WAY TO GRIP A PUTTER? HOW SHOULD MOST GOLFERS PUTT?

ANSWER:

I think there are a million different ways to grip a putter and putt, regardless if you putt cross-handed or use a conventional or long putter. My dad always told me to do whatever felt the most comfortable, and that's my suggestion to you.

Chapter 2 lets you compare some of the important positions of our four strokes. You'll see different grips, setup positions and even stroke planes. But we share something in common—a putter head that is square to the target line.

Chapter 3 and Martin Hall's drills will help correct some of the basic problems to get your stroke back on target.

—JIM

PRO: ROCCO MEDIATE

QUESTION: HOW DIFFICULT IS IT TO USE A LONG PUTTER?

ANSWER:

When I switched to the long putter, it took awhile to feel comfortable. Learning technique and improving your stroke will take about the same amount of time as learning to use a conventional putter.

What can you learn from me if you choose not to use a long putter? Although we may use different techniques, learning how to read a putt for both speed and accuracy is something I will help you with in Chapters 4 and 5.

As you look at the four of us in the same positions in Chapter 2, you will see how quiet our lower bodies are while putting. This is because *all* good putters use their shoulders and upper bodies while keeping their lower bodies virtually motionless.

—ROCCO

PRO: LEE JANZEN

QUESTION: HOW DO YOU DETERMINE PROPER PUTTING SPEED?

ANSWER:

We play several practice rounds early in the week and putt to where experience tells us the hole locations will be during the tournament. If you play most of your rounds on the same course, your mind subconsciously already has a good idea of the speed of your greens. The key is to think primarily about speed and not mechanics when you play.

Subtle terrain changes are also important when determining speed. I walk alongside my putting line toward the hole, allowing my feet to tell me about the terrain. If the putt is slightly uphill or downhill, your feet send out a balance signal to the brain.

We have other TOUR tips on reading putts for both speed and accuracy in Chapters 4 and 5.

— *LEE*

PRO: DAVE STOCKTON

QUESTION: DO YOU CHOOSE AN INTERIM TARGET ALONG THE TARGET LINE?

ANSWER:

My answer will surprise most people who look for an interim target farther down the target line. My target is less than an inch in front of the ball!

Picking a spot that close lets me see the ball roll over it. In fact, after taking my last look at the hole, my eyes return to that spot instead of the ball. Prematurely lifting my head is eliminated because the ball is already rolling to the hole when I next see it.

I'll explain more, along with additional suggestions to improve your accuracy, in Chapter 4. Martin Hall's Practice Green Drills at the end of each swing position in Chapter 2 will also help you work on your accuracy.

— *DAVE*

PRO: JIM FURYK

QUESTION: HOW DO YOU PLUMB BOB?

ANSWER:

Plumb bobbing is something I do to get a rough idea of how the ball will break. I'll demonstrate how this technique works in Chapter 4.

Plumb bobbing requires using your dominant eye and shutting the other. I'll also help you determine which is your dominant eye. Do you know which is your dominant one? Mine is my left eye.

Techniques like this are useful only when you know your putting mechanics will get the ball rolling along your intended target line. We help you eliminate some common mistakes in Chapter 3. For consistent putting, correct ball position is an example of something to replicate every time.

— JIM

PRO: ROCCO MEDIATE

QUESTION: DO YOU USE MENTAL IMAGES TO HELP YOU PUTT?

ANSWER:

Jack Nicklaus, before initiating his stroke, likes to see the ball roll all the way *into* the hole and then come *out* of the hole and roll back to his putter. History shows: That has worked great for him.

My visual image involves dumping a pail of water around the hole. The direction the water runs off is the direction the ball will roll. Chapter 4 includes tips to develop a positive mindset of seeing the ball rolling into the hole.

Some of the practice putting games in Chapter 8 will also help you develop confidence. Confident putters are good putters.

— ROCCO

2 ELEMENTS OF THE STROKE

"All I can do is start it. The good Lord handles it from there."—Jimmy Demaret

If one perfect putting method existed, everyone would be doing it. Instead, personal preference is the rule. With that in mind, this section will show a comparison of the various techniques, positions, alignments, grips and stroke planes employed by our four PGA TOUR experts.

The putting stroke can be broken down into six components: (1) address; (2) takeaway; (3) backstroke path; (4) pre-impact; (5) impact; and (6) follow-through.

Address is the only static or motionless component. Look at the others as waypoints on your stroke's uninterrupted journey.

Unlike the fluid centrifugal force generated by the full swing, the putting stroke is firm and purposeful, with very few moving parts. The key is to consistently deliver a clubface that is square to the target line at impact.

Let's go inside the ropes for a close-up look.

"You have to putt in a way that is naturally comfortable for you."—Jim Furyk

ABOUT THIS SECTION

In this section you will see our four professionals using their various stroke techniques, along with their comments about what they are feeling and doing in each position. Understanding is the initial step to learning. By comparing their strokes, you will be on your way to forming a positive approach for your own putting improvement.

• You will see each pro completing each of the six stroke components. You will see all the pros before advancing to the next position. This makes it easy to compare what each player is doing in that position.

• You will see close-up views of each component, both head-on and from behind.

• Pros' comments and added graphics help you work on your own stroke.

• At the conclusion of each stroke component, Martin Hall demonstrates some outstanding drills to help you master that phase of the stroke. Some of these Practice Green drills can be done at home with items you have around the house. These sections of the book make great references if something begins to go wrong with your stroke.

A NOTE ON MOTION

Always think of your putting stroke in terms of motion—not the static positions that we have broken it into for instructional purposes. Periodically glance back to previous positions and keep the motion of the entire stroke in proper perspective.

ADDRESS

The television cameras dramatically zoom in to reveal each precise movement of the victorious final putt. As the tension mounts, the eventual winner confidently and purposefully addresses the ball.

Is he thinking about mechanics at this crucial time? Or is his head filled with negative thoughts that will disrupt his concentration? Neither! He is focused on only one objective: rolling the ball into the hole.

Our four professionals frequently find themselves in tension-filled situations. And whether these pros use a cross-handed grip, a long putter or open or closed alignments, their approach is the same: return the putter head square to the target line at impact, sending the ball rolling toward the hole.

There is something to be learned from each approach to putting. Then Martin Hall demonstrates some drills to help you perfect your address position.

ADDRESS: LEE JANZEN

A s we analyze my putting stroke, pay particular attention to how my arms hang down below my waist as I grip the putter. When I first joined the PGA TOUR, it was evident to me that all great putters shared this one trait. I noticed that the guys who were not known as good putters held their hands high, which I think promotes an inconsistent, wristy-type stroke.

The farther your arms hang down, the more likely you will use them and your shoulders in the stroke, instead of your wrists. Hanging arms also ease tension.

Having said this, Dave Stockton, one of the game's greatest putters, prefers to hold his hands high. The message here: Try both styles and see which works best for you.

My head is lined up with the ball. In Chapter 4 we show how to determine your dominant eye. Mine is my left. That's the eye I want directly over the ball.

Notice my hands hang down below my waist, while Dave (left) prefers his higher. He begins his stroke with a forward press, while I prefer a one-piece takeaway.

Dave is not really wristy as he putts because he maintains the forward press angle through his stroke. His high hand position works for him. My lower hands work for me.

I place both thumbs flat on top of the putter grip to create a sense of feel. My hands are close together. My tendency is to hold the putter too loosely, so I have to remind myself to hold it tighter.

My ball position is in the middle of my stance. The hands are slightly ahead of the ball.

ven though I prefer to hang my arms below my waist, you'll notice, as you look at this photo, I'm gripping the putter high on the grip. The reason is my putter is shorter than most. My shaft length is only 32 inches. Dave's is a more conventional 34 to 35 inches.

As you look at our address positions, our foot alignment should stand out. While our shoulders, arms and hips are parallel to the target line, our foot alignment is not. We will explain our reasoning for this preference in Chapter 3.

All good putters prefer to have their eyes directly over the ball in order to see the target line better.

My weight is over the center of both feet as I bend from the waist. This posture position helps maintain a quiet lower body throughout the stroke.

My shoulders, arms, hips and knees are aligned parallel to the target line. How these body parts are lined up dictates your stroke. Setting up correctly every time is a proven formula for consistency.

Even though my feet are slightly open to the target line, I would prefer that they were parallel. But I notice over time that my tendency is to get them a little open.

My putter is at a 90-degree, or square, position to the target line. This is how the ball and putter head must meet at impact if I want to hole the putt.

ADDRESS: DAVE STOCKTON

As I set up to my target line, my thoughts are solely on feel, not mechanics. Once I have my line, I want to feel the speed the ball needs to roll. Work on mechanics only during a practice session.

Your address position needs to be comfortable. As we progress through my positions, I'll note helpful pointers that you can incorporate into your technique.

From this face-on view, notice that my head is lined up with the ball. You need to see a clear path to the hole down your target line. Tilting or cocking your head takes your eyes off the proper line.

My right hand is my feel, or power, hand. Pay close attention to the angle formed by the back of my right wrist and hand.

My left hand is my direction hand, guiding the putter on the correct path.

My legs are solid throughout the stroke. Sixty percent of my weight is on my side closest to the hole. I feel my weight on the balls of my feet.

The width of my stance varies, depending on what is comfortable for the terrain and how hard I plan on rolling the ball.

My left toe is pointed slightly inward, which allows me to maintain a solid position.

The ball is positioned inside my left foot, but it can be as far back as the middle of my stance. It depends on feel and the putt.

The advantage of this personalized instruction is that we can show you two views of each position, something you seldom see on television. We all customize certain components in our strokes. This view from behind, along with my explanation, illustrates a lot about my putting.

My head is aligned with the target line. Notice my chin is raised, instead of tucked into my chest. Don't slump your shoulders because that crimps your arms.

I bend at the waist and keep my back as straight as possible. I maintain my balance over the balls of my feet, keeping the steady position I need to putt successfully.

Keep your eyes over the ball. I want my eyes on the target line. I'm not looking at the ball, but at a spot directly in front of it on the line.

A word about knee flex: find a happy medium. Tall golfers need more flex, but they must be careful not to bend too much. Standing stiff legged or slightly flexed may improve your view of the target line, but it also can encourage incorrect lower body movement.

After taking my last look, and before initiating the stroke, my eyes return to that spot. I do not see the ball again until it rolls over it.

My hands are set high at address.

I prefer to have my feet slightly open. I do this by pulling my left foot back from the target line. My shoulders and hips remain parallel to the target line. This provides a better look at the target line, and the body does not get in the way of the stroke. My left direction hand will not be blocked as it guides the putter down the line.

The putter face and the target line must be at a 90-degree angle at address if you want them to be square at impact.

ADDRESS: JIM FURYK

I putt cross-handed. For a right-hander, this means my left hand is lower on the club than my right hand.

My left eye is my dominant eye, so I position my head at address where my left eye is on line with the ball.

I'm a square-to-square putter, which means I keep the blade on the target line throughout the stroke.

I use a pendulum stroke. You will see this in its various positions by watching the relationship of the triangle formed by my shoulders, chest, arms and hands.

With the exception of my feet, my body is aligned parallel to the target line. You need to set up parallel to roll the ball on line to the hole. Pay particular attention to your forearms.

The width of your stance is a comfort decision. There is no hard rule.

My weight is almost evenly distributed, slightly favoring my left foot. You should never place more weight on your back foot.

Some believe a cross-handed grip is more consistent because the hand positions make it harder for the stroke to break down. I've putted this way since I began playing, so I can't provide an honest comparison. I only know that it works for me.

As my stroke progresses, notice the constant angle formed by both wrists.

A grip key for me is to get my hands as close together as possible. I use both hands throughout the stroke. I don't think of one hand as being dominant.

DAVE SAYS

Compare my conventional grip (inset) with Jim's cross-handed grip (main photo). This is an example of how good putters can differ in approach. The key is that we both feel comfortable and confident to consistently roll the ball into the hole.

My ball position depends on how I want the ball to roll. Because I take my blade back low and then go up past impact, the best ball position for me is about one-third of the way back in my stance.

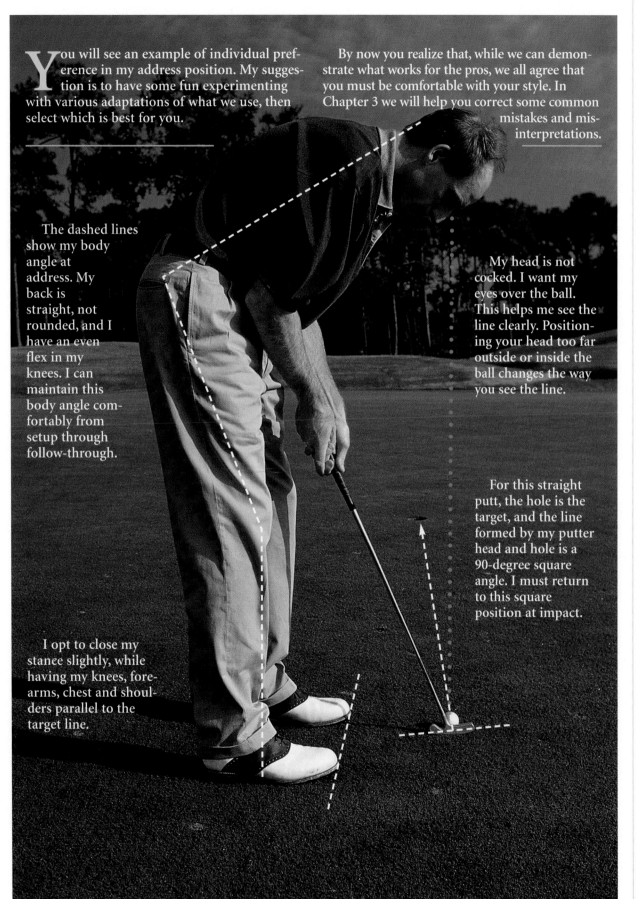

You will see an example of individual preference in my address position. My suggestion is to have some fun experimenting with various adaptations of what we use, then select which is best for you.

By now you realize that, while we can demonstrate what works for the pros, we all agree that you must be comfortable with your style. In Chapter 3 we will help you correct some common mistakes and misinterpretations.

The dashed lines show my body angle at address. My back is straight, not rounded, and I have an even flex in my knees. I can maintain this body angle comfortably from setup through follow-through.

My head is not cocked. I want my eyes over the ball. This helps me see the line clearly. Positioning your head too far outside or inside the ball changes the way you see the line.

For this straight putt, the hole is the target, and the line formed by my putter head and hole is a 90-degree square angle. I must return to this square position at impact.

I opt to close my stance slightly, while having my knees, forearms, chest and shoulders parallel to the target line.

ADDRESS: ROCCO MEDIATE

I prefer a long putter because it allows me to stand tall, unlike the conventional putters used by Lee, Dave and Jim. Because of my history of back problems, that is the big advantage.

On the PGA TOUR, if you can't practice putting, you're done! My back won't stand up to extended practice sessions. The long putter allows me to be competitive and win on the PGA TOUR.

My shoulders control the entire stroke. I use a pendulum stroke. Observing my shoulder line at the various positions will show you how to become a more accurate putter, even if you use a conventional putter.

With the long putter, I keep my thought process simple. I only think of my left shoulder on the backstroke and my right shoulder on the downstroke.

Notice how the butt of the club is positioned against my sternum. Some long putters use their chin or circle their hand around the top of the grip, but I feel this technique works better.

I place my right hand on the grip as I would a conventional putter. Some use their right hand as a claw.

My knees and shoulders are aligned parallel to the target line, but not my feet.

This is my normal width. If the wind is really blowing, I widen my stance for more stability. My foot line is slightly closed.

I feel my weight is evenly balanced, although there's slightly more on my left side.

The best ball position for me is off my left heel. Many putts are missed because of inconsistent ball positions.

This down-the-line view shows the major posture difference between a long putter and a conventional putter. Every time I ask myself why I use a long putter, I only need to look at the photo of Jim (right) bent over to answer the question. The 48-inch shaft in my putter allows me to stand tall so I can practice longer. Having used it competitively since 1991, I feel it gives me a bit of an edge.

Jim Furyk putts with a conventional 35-inch putter.

I'm standing as straight as I can, with only a slight bend at the waist. That is the purpose of a long putter. I'm perfectly balanced, with my weight over the center of my feet.

With a long putter you can't have everything. For instance, I have to align my eyes on the inside of the ball. When you stand tall, your eye line is naturally to the inside. I would have to contort myself into an unbalanced position to get my eyes over the ball.

I'm putting on a hole you see every year during THE PLAYERS Championship. It's the 18th hole on the Stadium Course at the Tournament Players Club of Sawgrass. Even though my foot line is slightly closed, my shoulders and knees are parallel to the target line.

My feet are slightly closed to the target line. They are the same during my golf swing, so it all blends together.

My putter head is square to the target line, forming a 90-degree angle. In this case, the target line and the line to the hole are the same. On breaking putts, align yourself to the line you want the ball to start on, instead of the line to the hole.

PRACTICE GREEN

Welcome to the Practice Green. I have some drills to help improve your putting. I'll employ a few training aids to help you develop correct mental images of what we are working on.

As with all aspects of the game, a good putt begins with a good grip. This is a part of your putting address that you can easily develop and practice at home.

PARALLEL ALIGNMENT GRIP

You need to grip the club so that you can draw a line across your forearms and shoulders that will be parallel to the target line. The common mistake is having these lines point left of the target line.

PARALLEL

INCORRECTLY POINTED LEFT

For this straight putt, the bar across my forearms is parallel to the target line from the ball to the hole. For breaking putts, the bar should be parallel to the line the ball starts on.

If your grip causes forearm alignment to point left, you must correct it. To check this on the practice green, have a friend hold a club on your forearms and tell you which way it's pointed.

HIGH-IN-THE-PALM GRIP

It's important for right-handers to grip the putter high in the palm of the left hand (high in the right hand if you putt left-handed). This gets the wrists high and facilitates a straight back-straight through stroke. Have your palms face each other so they can work in tandem.

HIGH PALM GRIP

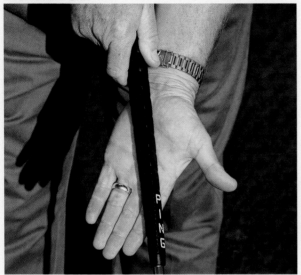

Putting grips with flat sides encourage facing palms. I begin by placing the grip in the palm of my left hand instead of in the fingers.

THUMB POSITION

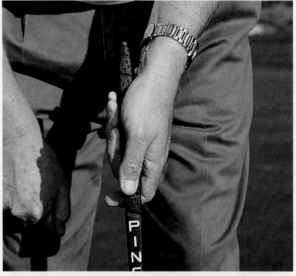

My left thumb is on top of the shaft. My palm position allows the back of my hand to point along the target line.

PALM FACING PALM

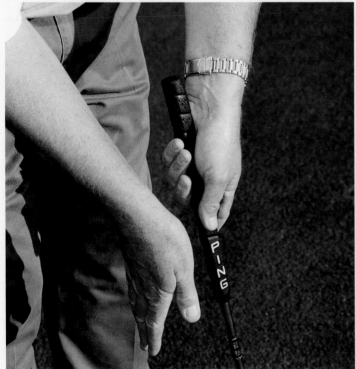

I bring my right hand toward the club. The palm is facing the left hand.

Facing palms ensure that my forearms set up parallel to the target line. My right thumb is on top of the shaft.

Elements
of the
Stroke:
Address

KEEP HANDS HIGH

Gripping the putter the way I demonstrated, you will notice your wrists have a natural arch, allowing you to hold your hands higher. While no stroke can ever be straight-back and straight-through, this high hand position keeps it closer to the target line.

The lower your hands, the more stroke arc you will see. The putter goes back more to the inside and, for some players, returning to a square impact position can be difficult. The result is inconsistency.

HANDS UP = BACKSTROKE CLOSER TO THE LINE

My hands are up at address and the shaft is more vertical. My backstroke is closer to the line. You need a more upright putter to help maximize this position.

HANDS LOWER = MORE INSIDE ARC

My hands are lower and closer to the body, while the shaft is less vertical. My backstroke results in an arc away and inside of the target line. The putter must return on this exact arc to impact the ball square to the target line.

TAKEAWAY

Have you seen your stroke on video? If it resembles an action adventure film, with lots of moving parts, you get a bad review.

Just as a film's director exerts creative control over a project, the *first* movement beginning the backstroke can direct the outcome of your putting stroke.

How each of our four TOUR professionals initiates his stroke—the takeaway—is the subject of this chapter. And this element of the stroke varies too, as you discovered with each address position.

To help groove your putting stroke with the skill and precision you need to lower your putts-per-round average, Martin Hall demonstrates a few excellent drills.

TAKEAWAY: LEE JANZEN

My putting stroke is a mini-version of my golf swing. At least, I think of it in those terms to get it started.

Think of the takeaway in terms of moving the triangle formed by the shoulders, arms and hands. This unified movement does not encourage a lot of separate hand motion. Here are some more things to consider in this position.

My head remains steady.

The triangle formed by my shoulders, arms and hands moves back together. Notice my hands remain slightly ahead of the putter as they move back from the ball.

As you continue to check my stroke positions, keep an eye on the angles formed by my wrists.

KEEP THE PUTTER HEAD LOW

My putter head remains close to the ground throughout my stroke. This is a blend of using my shoulders and hands.

You don't see much movement when you compare this view to the same view of me at address. That's the whole idea. All moving parts are purposely limited to the essentials.

As the putter head goes back, my swing plane becomes visible. The shaft is at an angle, not just vertical, so as I swing back my path will not be straight back. It's going to be a little curved.

My dominant left eye remains over the ball.

The posture angles I set at address will not change during my stroke. Unlike a full swing, my weight will not be transferred. This posture position helps me remain quiet throughout the stroke, eliminating any chance of having the club go off line.

The putter head is about square as it goes back, but this will slightly change as I reach the back of the stroke. The tilted shaft creates a natural arc back and through.

TAKEAWAY: DAVE STOCKTON

I think of myself as a wrist/feel putter. My initial movement is a forward press as the clubhead goes back. It's not two different motions; rather, I combine the two into one blended motion.

My putter has 5 degrees of loft. Most putters have 3 degrees. As I forward press, the loft decreases. If I started out with 3 degrees, I would have negative loft as I forward press, driving the ball into the ground at impact. I'll explain more about loft in Chapter 4.

Maintaining a steady head is important throughout my stroke. I'm still looking at the spot in front of the ball and will continue to do so until the ball rolls over it.

As my hands press slightly forward toward my left leg, the clubhead goes back. The cocking of my wrists creates a cupping of the right wrist. I maintain this position throughout my stroke.

My legs have not moved as the stroke begins. I keep them firm.

FORWARD PRESS DECREASES CLUBHEAD LOFT

Notice how the loft of the putter head decreases from the address position (top) as I forward press, taking the clubhead back in a simultaneous and seamless movement (bottom). Normal putter heads average 3 degrees of loft, but mine is 5 degrees. I would have negative loft at impact without the extra 2 degrees of loft.

Not much has changed from my address position with the exception of the club going back. My alignment is the same and my balance point is still over the balls of my feet.

I can spot bad putters if I see their spikes from the front. This means their weight is on their heels and they are leaning back.

My posture remains the same as it was at address. Any unnecessary movement negatively affects putting accuracy, so everything not connected to the swinging arm motion stays quiet.

I don't worry about where my backstroke goes. Most good putters take the putter inside the target line. When I putted my best, I took my putter outside and then looped around.

My left foot is planted back from the target line, so my stance is slightly open to facilitate putting across my lower body. This becomes very important as my left (direction) hand guides the club through the ball.

TAKEAWAY: JIM FURYK

As you look at my stroke at the various positions, you will notice how my putter stays low to the ground on the backstroke. It eventually goes up after impact. This is very natural to me.

I want my stroke to be more square to the target line going back and through the ball, so you will not see an inside swing arc.

Just as in the full swing, the shoulder movement in putting has to occur around a solid center—a steady head. Any movement causes the putter to go off path.

The triangle, formed by my shoulders, arms and hands, takes the putter away from the ball. At this early stage the motion is slight, but notice how the putter has moved away.

THE PUTTER GOES BACK LOW

Notice how close to the ground my putter is at address (top) and as I initiate my stroke (bottom). It will stay low on the backstroke and downstroke, rising up only after impact.

This view provides a good look at my squared takeaway. Where Ben Crenshaw opens and closes the blade during his stroke, I keep it as square to the line as possible.

Weighting the putter head helps both of us achieve our objective. I prefer more of a face-balanced putter, while Ben likes one with the weight more on the heel to help swing it open and closed. Chapter 4 will help you select the correct putter for your game.

My posture remains the same as I maintain a steady position throughout my stroke.

At this position, many golfers would already have the club swinging to the inside. The toe would be open, just as in your full swing. Instead, I want to restrict that movement and keep the putter as square to the line as possible going back.

My stance is closed, but my shoulders and forearms are parallel to the target line.

TAKEAWAY: ROCCO MEDIATE

As you look at my stroke, see how my shoulders control the movement. It's a pendulum stroke, or as "pendulum" as you can get without having the shaft totally vertical.

The natural movement of the shoulders will take the putter back a little to the inside and return it square to the target line at impact, and then continuing a little back to the inside as I follow through.

My head has stayed in the same position as it was at address. Moving your head and making crucial putts are not compatible.

Think left shoulder on the backstroke and right shoulder on the downstroke. Here on the takeaway, my left shoulder goes slightly down and moves the club away from the ball.

The butt of the club is directly on my sternum. The movement comes from the shoulders. I'm not pulling the club back with my right hand.

CLUB STAYS LOW TO THE GROUND

As I initiate my shoulder movement, the putter moves away from the ball at address (top) and stays close to the ground (bottom). A common stroke fault is lifting the club back instead of swinging it.

This view will help you understand the relationship of the putter to the target line at takeaway. In my case, I'm not doing anything other than lowering my left shoulder to create the slight inward path the club is on.

This is not the same shoulder turn you have in a full swing, where the upper body rotates back and around. All good putters, regardless of the length of their putters, should keep their shoulders and forearms parallel to the target line throughout the swing. The slight inside path is a natural occurrence, not a planned route.

My posture is the same as it was at address. I continue to feel the weight over the balls of my feet in the same proportion as it was at address. You should not feel a weight shift when putting.

Notice the slight inside swing path. This will continue on the backstroke. But the club returns to a square position at impact.

My feet are slightly closed to the target line, while my shoulders, forearms and knees are parallel. This allows the putter to return square to the ball (and to the target line) at impact.

PRACTICE GREEN

Yes, putting strokes have swing planes—the path the putter takes going back and through the ball. The physics of the angle of the shaft, when the putter head is resting flat on the ground, creates this natural motion arc.

Here are some drills and teaching aids to help you get your stroke on the proper plane.

STROKE PLANE SETUP

With your putter flat on the green (below), the shaft angle is clearly visible. As you will learn in Chapter 4, putters are available with different lie angles to suit your style. Some putters are more vertically upright while others have a flatter or more angled appearance.

To improve, regardless of your technique, you must be correctly aligned to the target line for your stroke plane to be effective. Why? When all of your lines match, it's easier to swing the club on plane and impact the ball with the squared face.

ALIGN TO THE PLANE

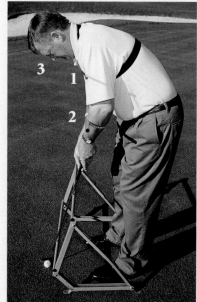

All good putters have their (1) shoulders, (2) arms and (3) eyes parallel to the plane line. Notice my feet are not parallel. In this section, the pros said that having your feet parallel to the target line is immaterial as long as the other body parts are properly aligned, and I agree.

EYES ALIGNED

I adjusted this teaching aid to show my swing plane angle. The shaft resting on it helps me align myself to the target line. You would think my stroke is straight back and through, but as you see in the next chapter, it arcs slightly.

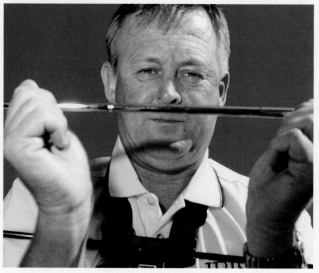

Your eyes must also be parallel to the target line so you can properly see the path the ball will start out on.

EYE POSITION

Ben Crenshaw, one of the best putters ever, definitely does not put his eyes directly over the ball. His eyes are inside the line, between the body and the ball.

In theory, if your eyes are inside the line, some people say you will push the putt to the right. And if your eyes are outside the line, you will pull the ball to the left. This is not always the case, but if you were building the optimum stroke, you would want your eyes over the line but not necessarily over the ball.

EYE POSITION CHECK

For these photos, I've hung a weighted ball on a string, but you can tie anything to the end of a line for weight. Address the ball, and let the weight hang from your eyeline down. Both photos show my eyes are on the target line. My head is slightly behind the ball; that's okay.

Elements of the Stroke: Takeaway

FOOT ALIGNMENT

As long as your shoulders, arms and eyes align your stroke plane to the target line, your foot position is a matter of personal preference. Here are three examples for you to try and compare the results.

The feet are parallel to the target line. You seldom see a pro in this parallel stance, but use it to compare the other two alignment suggestions. If it works best for you, then stick with it.

LEFT FOOT BACK

This position is used by Dave Stockton, Jack Nicklaus and Greg Norman among others. More good players putt with an open stance—the left foot slightly back from the line. It provides a slightly better view of the target line. With your left foot out of the way, you can look at the line a little better.

RIGHT FOOT BACK

This is the position used by Gary Player, Nick Faldo and the legendary Bobby Locke. This closed stance is ideally suited for putters who like to put a little hook spin on their putts.

BACKSTROKE PATH

Dave Stockton believes the backstroke is the least important part of the stroke. His rationale: "Moving the putter head down the line and impacting the ball in a squared position is all that matters."

This works for a player who is recognized internationally as an expert on putting. But do middle- and high-handicap golfers need a more grooved backstroke to set the club on the best possible track for the forward stroke? If you pull or push your putts, the answer is probably "yes."

As you improve your mechanics, muscle memory will eventually create a new natural backstroke path. If lowering your putts-per-green is your objective, consistently stroking on plane has its advantages.

Martin Hall demonstrates some stroke plane drills at the end of the chapter. But first we'll look at the pros' putting backstrokes.

BACKSTROKE PATH: LEE JANZEN

My stroke is a blend of shoulder and hand movements. Attaining consistent results from the 15- to 20-foot range requires more than the shoulders doing the work, so I also use my hands to create feel.

For comparison purposes, some of my backstroke photos will be inserted alongside the other pros, to help you see the differences in our four strokes. The differences are easy to spot, but to improve your putting, look for the similarities in our techniques.

My dominant left eye is still lined up with the ball, even as I have reached the back of my stroke path. Your eyes should be focused on the ball instead of following the moving club.

A comparison of my wrist angles at takeaway (small photo at right) and this position shows the angles have changed. This is the first visual evidence of my blended stroke.

My shoulders and arms stay connected, forming a triangle that moves the club away from the ball. My hands have also moved somewhat independently.

A pure shoulder (pendulum) putter maintains the same wrist angles all the way back, but I've incorporated slight hand movement, and the angles reflect that. This hand movement provides the feel I need.

I putt best when the club stays low to the ground. The reason: The club follows a natural stroke arc as a result of the unified triangle swinging back. The common mistake of lifting the club, instead of swinging it, takes the putter off line and immediately off the ground.

My body remains still during my backstroke. A weight shift is not needed for this short stroke.

At this stage of my stroke, my job is to allow my sense of feel to take control of how far I take the club back. The only visible change in this photo from the previous takeaway view is the club path. My stroke is that quiet.

Do I need to change my spine angle or move my head or transfer my weight? Absolutely not!

I'm not purposely swinging the club back slightly to the inside of the target line either. That is a natural occurrence of my unified triangle movement. When my club returns to the ball, it will be square to the line at impact.

My head remained steady and my eyes are over the target line.

My posture remains the same as it was at address. Only the body parts necessary to keep the club swinging along the correct plane are moving.

The putter head followed the stroke plane, which is slightly inside the target line. Thinking in terms of a full golf swing, the club should go slightly inside on the backstroke and then square an inch or two prior to impact.

This slightly open stance provides a better view of the target line than a parallel stance. I would prefer to be square, but I get open naturally.

BACKSTROKE PATH: DAVE STOCKTON

I don't worry where my backstroke goes. Most good putters, like Billy Casper, take the putter inside. When I putt my best, the putter comes back outside the target line, which is unusual, and then loops around for the return.

I'm not one to take the putter straight back and straight through either. My real focus is the path the putter takes going down the path toward the target. The "back of the left hand drill" I demonstrate in Chapter 4 helps achieve that goal.

Every good putter keeps a steady head during the stroke. My eyes are still over the ball, but keep in mind they are focusing on a target line spot less than an inch in front of the ball.

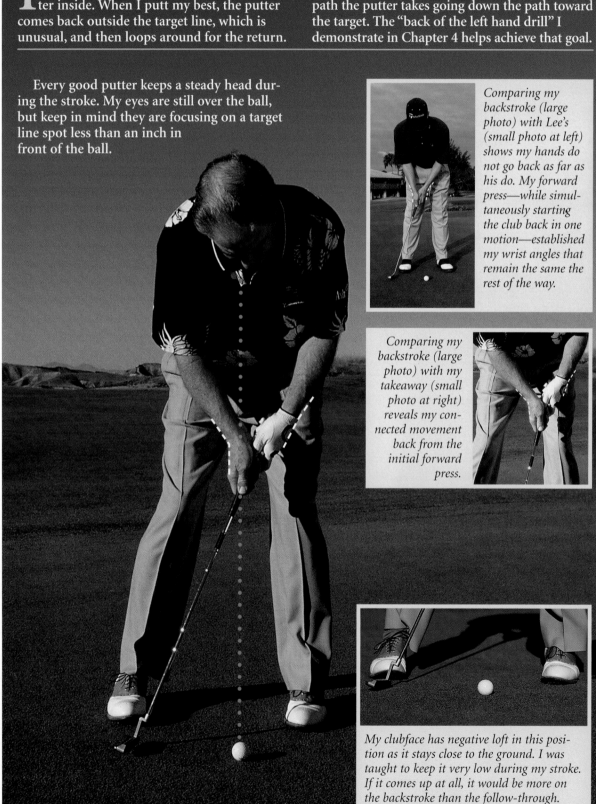

Comparing my backstroke (large photo) with Lee's (small photo at left) shows my hands do not go back as far as his do. My forward press—while simultaneously starting the club back in one motion—established my wrist angles that remain the same the rest of the way.

Comparing my backstroke (large photo) with my takeaway (small photo at right) reveals my connected movement back from the initial forward press.

My clubface has negative loft in this position as it stays close to the ground. I was taught to keep it very low during my stroke. If it comes up at all, it would be more on the backstroke than the follow-through.

If you are on slow greens and must roll the putt faster, the key is to make sure you accommodate the distance with your swing. This is where feel comes in.

A problem occurs if you take the same backswing and then accelerate to impact the ball. This causes popping. Your stroke needs to have a smooth rhythm all the way through.

The steady head remains over the ball.

Setting good posture angles at address allows you to maintain them comfortably during the stroke.

My path is slightly inside the line. As I mentioned earlier, this path is not as important to me as the path back to the ball.

BACKSTROKE PATH: JIM FURYK

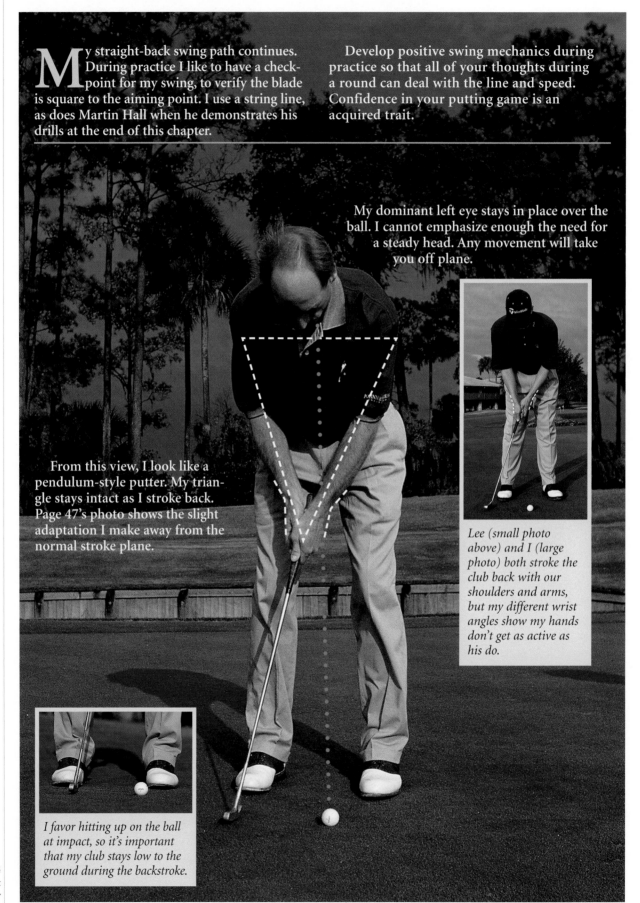

My straight-back swing path continues. During practice I like to have a checkpoint for my swing, to verify the blade is square to the aiming point. I use a string line, as does Martin Hall when he demonstrates his drills at the end of this chapter.

Develop positive swing mechanics during practice so that all of your thoughts during a round can deal with the line and speed. Confidence in your putting game is an acquired trait.

My dominant left eye stays in place over the ball. I cannot emphasize enough the need for a steady head. Any movement will take you off plane.

From this view, I look like a pendulum-style putter. My triangle stays intact as I stroke back. Page 47's photo shows the slight adaptation I make away from the normal stroke plane.

Lee (small photo above) and I (large photo) both stroke the club back with our shoulders and arms, but my different wrist angles show my hands don't get as active as his do.

I favor hitting up on the ball at impact, so it's important that my club stays low to the ground during the backstroke.

My straight path away from the ball is the most obvious difference when you compare my putting to the other players'. Simple physics has to be overcome for me to accomplish this.

If the club was more vertical, a pendulum movement would

naturally take it straight back and through, just like the pendulum in a grandfather's clock. But in my address the shaft is inclined, so a normal pendulum stroke would take it slightly inside ... unless I purposely keep it more on line, which I do.

Our postures may be different, but the similarity we share is how quiet we stay throughout the stroke. If your posture remains quiet, the clubhead can stay on plane.

We keep emphasizing it because it's so key: We keep our heads steady because the end result is holing more putts.

Notice how different this looks when compared to the other pros' stroke paths. Practice helps me work on attaining this straight-back position.

BACKSTROKE PATH: ROCCO MEDIATE

I don't believe a long putter is meant to be swung short. One thing I always think about is letting it swing wherever it wants to go. With a three-foot putt, I don't have to do that. But for 10- to 15-foot putts, it's more feel; the length of the swing happens naturally.

Aside from the obvious difference in putter lengths, I share some similarities with the other pros. Establishing good putting mechanics allows you to make the same swing consistently without having to think about it during crucial times—like during a high-pressure tournament.

My shoulders have moved but not my head! It remains the center, stable point of my stroke.

Left shoulder down clearly shows here. With the butt of the club against my sternum, only this shoulder motion is swinging the club back.

Although I use the long putter (large photo) and Lee (above) uses one that is shorter than regulation, we both maintain a unified and connected movement away from the ball. Our shoulders and arms stay linked in the same relative positions on the backstroke.

On the backstroke, my swing plane takes the putter head off the ground. As with most elements of my stroke, I allow this to happen naturally.

This position clearly shows the differences our swing paths take. My path is entirely different than Jim's. My suggestion is to work on making a unified and connected backstroke and downstroke while observing the path your club takes. Visualizing this helps you develop a positive mental image.

A slight inside stroke path is the more natural occurrence for me, but for comparison purposes, try taking it straight back and evaluate the results. You have to find the stroke that will work for you.

I wear sunglasses virtually all the time I play, to protect myself from harsh glare that can tire eyes (and your body) out. My eyes remain inside the ball and I haven't cocked my head.

My shoulders remain parallel to the target line as they swing back. The shaft angle is responsible for the inside swing path. An upper body turn *does not* generate this inside swing path. I maintain the same spine angle throughout the stroke.

A tilted pendulum stroke produces an inside putter head at this position. This is the natural swing path. When I return to the ball, the putter head will retrace the path and square up for impact.

PRACTICE GREEN

Many golfers are surprised to learn that staying on plane is as important to putting as it is to their full swing. Why would such a short stroke, which doesn't go up and around, have anything to do with a plane?

Have you come to the right place! Here are some drills to illustrate how your club follows a plane, and how to achieve that "just right" movement.

TOUCH THE ROPE DRILL

You can use a practice green, or even the backyard, to work on the basic aspects of this drill. You need about 15 feet of rope, a couple of stakes and a 2x4.

CREATE PARALLEL LINES

Select a straight putt, then draw an imaginary line through the ball to the target. Place the 2x4 parallel to the imaginary line. The 2x4 should be on the ground and outside the ball. Finally, stake the rope parallel to both lines and inside the target line.

SHAFT GENTLY TOUCHES ROPE

Place your putter with the sweetspot directly behind the ball. The shaft should just be gently touching the rope. Do not move the rope toward you, as in the small photo.

DISCOVER YOUR PLANE

Do not move the rope toward you or touch the 2x4. Then stroke back, sliding the shaft gently on the rope. The putter shaft stays on the rope but moves away from the 2x4. Your putter head just swung back on an inclined plane.

MOVING SHOULDER DRILL

Your stroke should start with the shoulders and arms. To develop this feeling, try this one-handed shoulder drill.

To begin, hold the putter in your right hand and place your left hand on your right shoulder.

The right shoulder should always be moving during the stroke. You want to feel the right shoulder move as you stroke back (top) and through (bottom).

PRE-IMPACT

Can you think of any important similarities in the transition phases of the full swing and putting stroke? The differences are certainly more obvious. Accurately propelling the ball a long distance requires winding and unwinding the torso, combined with timing elements that all come together at impact. The putting stroke must be motion-free with the exception of the shoulders, arms and hands.

But there are two important similarities. The accuracy of both shots depends on the clubface being square to the target line at impact. And the forward putting stroke, like the full swing, must consistently follow the stroke plane back to the ball, as seen in our four professionals' pre-impact positions.

Do they start their ball rolling with an upward or downward moving putter face? This pre-impact analysis provides the answers to these and other questions. Then Martin Hall continues his stroke plane drills.

PRE-IMPACT: LEE JANZEN

The pre-impact position is the spot where so many amateurs begin making a fatal putting mistake. The wrist flipping will begin as the hands incorrectly start releasing through the ball.

Instead of the angle retention you see in our strokes—with the cup in the right wrist and a flatter left wrist—wrist flippers look just the opposite as their putter leads the hands through the ball. Look for retained wrist angles in all our pre-impact positions.

If we sandwiched together all the photos of my stroke, you will see my head has remained in exactly the same position. Moving your head is one of the most common, but easily correctable, problems.

Does this give you the idea of how my shoulders, arms and hands move together as a single unit toward the ball? Putting with this visual image in your mind helps you stay on the correct swing plane.

These are the wrist angles I referred to at the top of the page. My right wrist is cupped while the left remains straighter. Maintain this relationship through impact.

As it returns toward impact, the putter skims slightly off the ground. The face is slightly angled down, indicating negative putter head loft. At impact, you'll see the reason for the extra loft milled into my head.

One of the problems I occasionally have is that my eyes sometimes make the putter follow my feet—a problem that surfaces most often when my stance is slightly open, as it seems to be most of the time.

The correction is to purposely close the stance so the right foot is back more. This changes my optics and puts me back on line.

One of the important posture lines to look at is the one connecting the back of my head to my lower back. After setting this line, I don't want any upward or downward movement with my upper torso. Check all of my positions. The angle of the line remains constant and my swing stays on plane.

Keep a steady head with your eyes over the ball. This is hard—I struggle with it, as mentioned above. Actually, my head is steady, but my peripheral vision causes the problem.

The path back toward the ball is the most important aspect of this position. My ball must start rolling on the correct line I selected to the hole. Accomplishing this goal requires my putter face arriving at a 90-degree angle to the target line about an inch or two behind the ball. This is the all-important square position.

PRE-IMPACT: DAVE STOCKTON

This position plays a pivotal role in going through the impact position solidly. The reason for my initial forward press is to begin with my hands ahead of the club, and as you can see here, I remain in that position.

My dominant left hand has the responsibility of starting this putt on the target line.

My head is fixed in its original address position. Even though my eyes are over the ball, they're fixed on a spot less than an inch in front of it. That's my interim target.

The back of my dominant left hand is pointing toward the target line.

My wrist angles formed when I initiated my swing with a forward press and simultaneously moved the club back. I'm a wrist/feel putter as a result of that movement. I want my big muscles to stay quiet so the feeling in my wrists and hands can propel the ball.

My legs could be encased in granite. That's how still they remain. Do not sway, pivot or create any lower body movement.

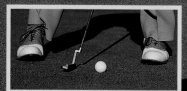

My putter remains low to the ground as it returns to the ball. The reason: My hands stay at the same level from the address position to follow-through. Combine this with a left hand going toward the hole, and you have the reason for my accuracy over the years.

Rolling the ball is what putting is all about. My wrist/feel method works very well for me. Wrist putters cock their wrists and then uncock them, causing the putter to come up instead of staying low.

Shoulder putters eliminate all wrist movement and consequently make longer strokes to compensate. You may find longer strokes are more difficult to be consistently effective in certain situations, like downhill putts. Work on feel to help take care of the distance challenges.

Solid as granite! A firm base, aided by good posture, eliminates many of the problems responsible for inconsistent impact positions.

My eyes are over the ball, but looking at a spot slightly in front of it on the target line. I want to see the ball rolling over that spot.

DAVE SAYS:

The major reason most people miss putts is because they don't read them correctly. Here are my suggestions:

• See your putt before stroking it.

• Before putting, see a highway to the hole and visualize exactly where the ball will fall in.

The putter approaches from slightly inside but stays low to the ground. My feet are open to allow room for the left hand to come through on target, but the rest of my body is parallel to the target line.

Elements of the Stroke: Pre-Impact

Just like Dave, I putt my very best when my club stays low and level. My stroke is low going back, so it favors hitting up on the ball.

Hitting on an upswing—and golfers have different theories about this—is something you really don't know you do unless you videotape your swing. I know that in my case a fairly level impact is best as the club approaches low.

My dominant left eye is directly over the ball. I'll demonstrate this later, but you find your dominant eye by:

1 Making a circle with your thumb and forefinger;

2 With one of your arms outstretched and both eyes open, center an object in the circle;

3 Open and close each eye. The one that still has the object centered is your dominant eye.

The triangle symbolizes the connection between the shoulders, arms and hands. Staying connected while moving only this triangle keeps you on the correct swing plane.

As the putter returns toward the ball, notice the angles formed by both wrists and how I've maintained them throughout my stroke. A cross-handed grip can help you keep your left wrist from breaking down at impact.

My putter is not descending toward the ball just before impact. Rather, it's arriving level. Overspin is a result of the blade going up past impact.

JIM SAYS:

My competitive golf has always been about getting to the next step. In high school I wanted to get ready for college, so I needed to play well to get recognized by the coaches.

My first year out of college I went to the TOUR school and earned my Nike TOUR card and won an event. The next year I went back to TOUR school, earning the coveted PGA TOUR card. Fortunately, winning was the next important step I took.

So far, you probably have noticed that a cross-handed putter's stroke is similar to the one used by a conventional putter. Having done this all my life, it seems natural for me.

Others say cross-handed putters have an advantage because their wrists do not break down during impact; they stay solid through the ball instead of getting all "wristy." Players turn to this technique when their styles have failed, so maybe it makes sense to start experimenting with a cross-handed grip under more positive circumstances. Evaluate its potential and see what you think.

I can't think of a reason to move around during your putting stroke. My parallel lines at address (for my shoulders, waist and knees) would be adversely changed and so would my swing path.

My eyes are still over the ball. Make this position as standard as you can. Getting too outside or inside the target lines changes the way you see the putt. You want to see it the same way all the time, every time.

By keeping my putter face on the target line during the backstroke, it returns square to the ball at this position. This putting preference works for me but I know it may be more reliable for you to have a slight inside arc. The choice is yours. Only practice and experimentation will help you decide.

PRE-IMPACT: ROCCO MEDIATE

Shoulders! Shoulders! Shoulders! If you want to use a long putter, think in those terms to simplify the stroke. Linking the shoulders and arms, and taking them back together, takes the entire package back before reversing the shoulder movement toward the ball.

Want an even better equation to work with? Less moving parts equals more holed putts. Long putter, conventional putter or even a short putter like my old Florida Southern teammate Lee Janzen uses … all professionals limit the movement to only the essentials.

My head position is in line with the ball, but as I explained earlier, not directly over it. That's the one trade-off for using a long putter. However, my eye position inside the line is still better than outside the line.

During the backstroke, my thought is "left shoulder back." On my downstroke, that changes to thinking "right shoulder through."

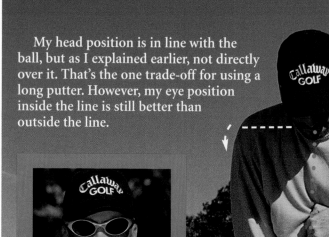

ROCCO SAYS:

Here's a tip to get your shoulders more into your stroke. Placing the ball off your left heel is a good spot in your setup and allows your shoulder muscles to do most of the work.

The bad putters you see among your friends are probably wristy and will have to *really* work to improve. And remember to keep your lower body still.

Dave Stockton is my model for having granite legs. His pants don't move and his putts go in!

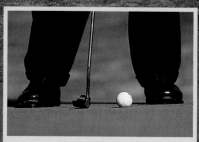

My club has returned to ground level as it approaches the ball. For some personal feedback, ask a friend to get down low and watch you putt, concentrating only on the putter height. Compare that information with our strokes.

Those of us who play professionally have a chance to work on our mechanics during practice sessions. If you have limited time to play, chances are you won't spend it on the practice range or green. You'll hit the fairways. So while we pros have the "luxury" of concentrating only on speed and feel once we have the putting line, you're thinking about mechanics. Big advantage to the pro!

Here's my suggestion: Work on putting mechanics at home. Grip, posture, address, takeaway and downstroke are all easily practiced and perfected away from the course. Some pros even practice mechanics in their hotel rooms.

I'll gladly trade this slightly inside-the-target-line eye position for the ability to stand up straight when I practice and putt. Being inside the line is far better than having your eyes outside the target line.

Being able to stand up straight like this has added years to my career. My back is functional and I'm still out there playing. Some players switch to the long putter for the yips, but I did it for the increased practice time.

I personally don't think your putter blade should ever go back straight and return straight through. It's easier and more consistent for most golfers to come a little inside going back, be square at impact, and then continue on to follow-through a little to the inside.

PRACTICE GREEN

The subjects of *steady head* and *solid lower body* were mentioned frequently in this chapter. As you work on improving your putting, use the drills on pages 60 and 61 frequently, to train yourself to stay quiet during the stroke.

BALL-ON-THE-EAR SHADOW DRILL

Your head needs to stay very still when you putt. This is a great drill to develop that feeling … as long as the sun is shining!

BALL ON LEFT EAR

Place a ball on the green and, with the sun at your back, line it up on the shadow of your left ear.

STEADY HEAD AS YOU STROKE

For this drill, keep your eye on your shadow and the ball. Stroke back and forth. Concentrate on keeping the ball on your shadow's ear. Once you train yourself to keep it properly positioned, you have successfully developed the feeling for maintaing a steady head throughout your stroke.

QUIET LOWER BODY DRILL

Practice this drill at home to train your lower body to remain quiet during the swing. Remember, Dave Stockton emphasized having legs of granite.

SET UP WITH AN EXTRA CLUB

LEGS OF GRANITE = DRIVER WILL NOT MOVE

As you set up to your putt, place a long club like your driver against your left thigh. Should you see the club move out of the corner of your left eye as you putt, your legs are moving.

Practice your putting stroke until the club doesn't move. For this drill, the ball is just for a visual reference.

Elements
of the
Stroke:
Pre-Impact

TWO-CLUB MOTION DETECTOR

Here is a bonus drill that will dramatically detect any undesirable lower body movement. You will need a bungie cord with hooks on both ends, and two clubs from your bag.

DRILL SETUP

(1) Hook one end of the bungie cord on a five-foot wooden dowel available from a home improvement store. (2) With the dowel resting on your upper legs, fasten the other hook around your legs and secure it. (3) Adjust the dowel on your upper thighs and rest a club at either end against the dowel. The key is not to move your lower body during the actual drill (below), because any movement causes a club to drop.

GOOD: SOLID LEGS DURING BACKSTROKE

The club will not fall if your legs remain solid and quiet during your backstroke.

BAD: BACKSTROKE LEG MOTION

If the right club falls, your lower body movement is probably causing you to push your putts to the right. Work on transforming your legs into solid granite pillars.

GOOD: SOLID LEGS ON FORWARD STROKE

The club will not fall if your legs remain solid and quiet during your forward stroke.

BAD: DOWNSTROKE LEG MOTION

If the left club falls, you are probably pulling your putts to the left. Work on transforming your legs into granite pillars.

IMPACT

Reducing your average putts-per-green translates into lower scores. Subtracting a half-stroke per green per round, for example, would save you nine strokes!

Obviously our four TOUR professionals don't hole every putt, but they seldom three-putt either. When they miss a putt, they usually leave a short putt back. Amateurs, especially those with haphazard stroke planes, struggle with 5- and 6-footers.

How important is returning your putter square to the target line at impact? You may have found the perfect line to the hole and determined the perfect speed. But unless the putter impacts the ball at a square 90-degree angle, start adding—not subtracting—strokes to your score.

Speed, and reading the line, play big roles in reducing scores. We'll cover those later. For now, with the aid of high-speed photography, it's time to look at impact. Martin Hall demonstrates some great impact drills too.

IMPACT: LEE JANZEN

My putting stroke is similar to my golf swing. I take it back under control, pause slightly, and then putt through. Think in those terms instead of hitting the ball. Putting with acceleration, rhythm and control, instead of trying to match the same stroke speed back and through, works for me.

The full-page photo below was taken a split-second after impact, and the small photo captures the exact moment the face contacted the ball. Both photos provide the opportunity to closely examine this crucial phase of my stroke.

My steady head is the anchoring point for the connected triangle of shoulders, arms and hands.

The role my shoulders play is obvious, as evidenced by the left shoulder riding slightly higher. The shoulders stay parallel to the target line but move as a unit with the arms.

The sense of feel in my blended stroke comes from my hands. As a result, slight changes can be detected in both wrist angles when compared with my pre-impact position; the hands adjust as the stroke continues.

Notice the parallel lines formed by my knee alignment and target line. When these lines (along with my shoulders) all point to the same direction, an online putt is the result.

If your putting is inconsistent, take a few moments and check your alignment. Pros are always working on alignment. My suggestion is to take this phase of putting very seriously!

Amazingly, you can see the exact moment of impact. Here's what you can tell from this photo:

- *The shaft is slightly forward of the ball, indicating my hands are ahead at impact.*

- *The putter face made contact in the level position I prefer, not on an upstroke or downstroke.*

- *The putter loft is about zero, but in a fraction of a second, with the ball still on the face, it will increase to lift the ball very slightly to start the roll.*

Even at impact you don't see changes in my posture, eye position or address. What you do see is a blade square to the target line at impact. The ball has no choice but to begin rolling along the line I selected toward the hole.

My eyes are still over the spot where the ball was. Now that we've reached impact, can you begin to appreciate the need to see the target line? In Chapter 3 we demonstrate how to check for eye position.

Stay in position! If you move prior to or at this putting position, disaster awaits. Earlier, I gave my reasons for hanging my arms down lower than most players. Maintaining this posture allows me to maximize the benefits.

Ninety degrees is the magic number. This is the squared position we've been telling you about. If you are off even slightly at impact, the ball will roll several feet offline.

IMPACT: DAVE STOCKTON

The ball is rolling over my target spot. Unlike other players who find an interim target several feet or more down their target line, mine is within an inch of my ball.

That's the spot I've been looking at during my stroke. Now at impact, I'm seeing the ball roll over that spot. As we help you read greens later in this book, I'll demonstrate some tips for finding your target line.

The ball is rolling directly over the spot I've been looking at during the stroke.

I've maintained these wrist angles through impact. This hooded down the loft of the putter face. But remember I have 5 degrees of loft built in my putter, compared to the normal 3 degrees. Retaining these angles keeps me from adding loft, and the putter arrives with 2 or 3 degrees of loft at impact.

The glove logo on my dominant left hand is pointing down the target line. The feeling is that I want to stroke the back of my hand over that spot. In Chapter 4 I'll demonstrate my drill to send your ball straight down the line.

Even one of our infamous California earthquakes won't make me move my legs during my putting stroke! I'm going to have legs of granite.

Notice how level and low my club remains at impact. Sometimes I'll take the putter back and get it stuck and be too lazy to start over. I have to accelerate through the putt.

As you look at this photo, notice how I stroke through the ball, allowing my dominant left hand to work down the target line. Now you see my reasoning for drop- ping my left foot back while the rest of my body remains parallel to the target line. Have some fun and experiment as you work on building your reliable putting stroke.

My posture has not changed. This is very important.

My line of sight is still on the spot the ball is rolling over. I know the view of the mountain range is beautiful here at the PGA of Southern California Golf Club, but the time to look up and admire it is after the ball goes in the hole.

The putter has arrived square to the target line at impact, led by my dominant left hand. I use both hands during my stroke. The right hand is for power and feel. The left hand is for leading the putter back to the ball.

IMPACT: JIM FURYK

The positions you see in these Elements of the Stroke sections are presented as an instructional view of our putting strokes. I'm not consciously thinking about the mechanics it takes to reach these specific waypoints during my stroke. They occur naturally as a result of my swing path.

As I putt, my only thoughts are about sending the ball off at the correct speed. Speed was determined earlier during my practice strokes as I programmed it into my mind.

All of us are saying the same thing about maintaining a steady head throughout the putting stroke. For a moment, let's compare the full swing to the putting stroke.

Even though I'm not a true pendulum putter, I still rely on the connected triangle to create the movement.

- The moving head moves the position of the bottom of your full swing arc. This results in a chunked or thin shot.

- Compensations trying to get back to the ball causes those problems.

Here, at the exact moment of impact, you can see my wrist angles have remained constant. My cross-handed grip restricts wrist flipping, and I'm stroking through the shot with my hands slightly ahead.

- Moving your head while putting also moves the body off the stroke arc. The club will still impact the ball, but the face will be open or closed, sending the ball off line.

My blade is coming up slightly past impact, imparting topspin on the ball.

ee and Dave prefer stances with their left foot back, while Rocco and I drop the right foot back. These are different strategies, but there is a common (and more important) denominator: No matter what our stance, the putter's blade is square to the target line at impact. This sends the ball off on the right line. No great mystery about it!

My spine and posture angles are exactly the same as they were at address. If my body stays quiet, I can stroke the blade square to the target line at impact.

My eyes are over the target line at impact. If my head stays quiet, it's another assurance that my blade will square up to the target line at impact.

Square to the target line is the end result of all the stroke elements:

- Address.

- Takeaway.

- Backstroke path.

- Pre-impact.

Sloppy setups or unnecessary movements along the way eliminate your ability to return the putter to the squared position—the one that starts your ball rolling on the target line.

IMPACT: ROCCO MEDIATE

The ball gets in the way of my pendulum stroke at impact. I'm not consciously trying to hit it. Once I take the club back, I just let it go along in tempo with my right shoulder.

Feel is something we talk about in this book, realizing that those of us who play virtually every day have a better sense of it than part-time players. You have to feel both the distance and the speed of your putt. My putter even has a sterling silver insert to increase my sense of feel.

So as important as all this stroke mechanics advice is, please give equal consideration to the speed drills and instruction we offer later in the book.

With Dave Stockton as my model for stability, there is no way I would move my head at impact.

At impact my shoulder line is fairly level because of my right-shoulder-through-stroke philosophy for the forward movement. Even if you use a conventional putter, try thinking left-shoulder-back for your backstroke and right-shoulder-through for the downstroke.

My putter is still low to the ground slightly past impact. At follow-through it rises, following the stroke path.

It worked! My putter face is square to the target line here at impact. Golf looks so easy when you watch professionals play, but you seldom see all the hours we spend practicing.

Our long practice sessions maintain our skill levels. If your putting is even slightly off, you won't last long out on the TOUR.

My eyes are inside the ball but still provide an accurate view of the target line. Remember that it's better for your eyes to be aligned inside of the line rather than outside.

Standing up makes it easier to maintain my address posture and angles. Even long putters need to remain in place to putt consistently.

The yellow line shows the path my putter head followed to return to the squared position for impact. Inclined shafts follow an inside plane back and through.

PRACTICE GREEN

Having just seen the impact positions of our four professionals and read their comments, you now understand the importance of arriving square to the target line at impact.

Let's begin our drills with a visual demonstration on how to start your ball rolling on the highway to the hole. The pros refer to this position as impact, but I prefer to call it contact.

VISUALIZING THE HIGHWAY-TO-THE-HOLE

Using this golf ball with a center tire tread around it will help you understand why your clubhead must be square when it contacts the ball.

At contact the putter meets the ball/tire square to the target line, sending it rolling straight down the highway to the hole. If the putter arrives at an angle, the ball/tire would go off the road. Square is the only way to make the ball roll along the target line.

SQUARE FACE CONTACT DRILL

This is a simple drill to help you bring a square face back to the ball. All you need are two tees and a ball.

HIT BOTH TEES

After you stroke back (4), return the club to the ball (5), trying to knock both tees down at the same time.

- *Both tees knocked down = square clubface.*

- *Heel tee knocked down first = open clubface at contact.*

- *Toe tee knocked down first = closed clubface at contact.*

DRILL SETUP

Position your putter on the ground and place a tee at the toe (1). Place another tee touching the heel of the putter (2), and finally place the golf ball in the center of the tees (3).

FOLLOW-THROUGH

The follow-through is the most overlooked component of the putting stroke. The ball has already started rolling toward the hole, so how can the follow-through affect it? Our four TOUR professionals realize how vital good follow-through is.

How you finish your stroke affects...

- The target line stroke path.

- The spin placed on the ball at impact.

- The speed of the putt.

While not as dramatic as a full-swing finish, putting follow-through is a major contributor to accuracy and speed. Any deviation from the swing path in this position means the change was made prior to impact, which results in a violation of our "be square" rule.

Let's see how the pros follow through. Then, always at the ready, Martin Hall will be waiting on the Practice Green with drills to help you finish successfully.

FOLLOW-THROUGH: LEE JANZEN

The triangle and ball moved. That's about all you can see in this photo. Or is it? Absence of movement is equally important to becoming a good putter. This sounds simple and easy, but chances are you move.

Several helpful drills are featured in this section. Applying them helps curtail non-essential body movements. Review our body positions and keep them in mind as you practice. Address the ball with the proper posture and alignment, stay connected, and stroke back and through.

Following through to the hole is the one dominant thought I have at this stage. You see it as I slightly reach out with the putter.

LEE SUGGESTS:

In Chapter 3 we'll help you identify some of your stroke problems and offer suggestions to correct them. If you have limited practice time, putting mechanics can be worked on at home in front of a mirror.

Use the practice putting green to work on speed and feel before teeing off. The mechanics you worked on at home increase your confidence.

The club rises up past impact. This follow-through motion puts topspin on the ball to help keep it on line.

I want my putter to be square an inch or two before impact and continue to be square an inch or two past impact. You see that happening on this page. The ball is tracking perfectly on my intended line.

My head and eye positions do not offer telltale clues to my stroke positions. They will look the same at address and impact. Head movement is a problem you already know how to correct by using Martin Hall's drill.

The ball left the clubface, so it's safe for me to move. But I'm not moving. The reason: I'm still concentrating and feeling this putt as I stroke through it.

My clubhead appears square to the target line just past impact as I'm following through to the hole.

FOLLOW-THROUGH: DAVE STOCKTON

Throughout the forward stroke, the direction was led by my dominant left hand. The back of the hand will stroke over my target spot an inch down the target line.

How do I determine the length of my back-stroke and follow-through? I was taught never to leave a putt short, but rather finish 16 inches past the hole. Once I visualize my highway to the hole, feel takes over and regulates the length of my stroke.

I'm still looking at the target spot. If your head comes up to look at the rolling ball too early, try focusing on a spot just an inch from your ball on the target line. Once you see the ball roll over that spot you can jump up and down if you want since the ball is already on its way.

DAVE SUGGESTS:

I divide every putt into thirds. In the first third the ball is going its fastest and won't be affected by the break. In the second third the break will start to come into play, and in the last third the putt will break more.

I'm more interested in the break around the hole than the break that's immediately around the ball.

The wrist angles have slightly changed, but, as you can see, the back of my hand is still pointing down the target line.

The photo proves my putter remains low after impact. The reason: my left hand stays low going toward the target.

I was taught my right hand is my power or feel hand, and the left is the direction hand. As you look at my follow-through, notice that my left wrist goes down and through rather than up.

If a club comes up, it may put topspin on the ball, but your direction may be adversely affected. In Chapter 4 I'll demonstrate a drill to help you keep your follow-through low.

Have you noticed any change in my posture in this photo? Good for you. I haven't moved yet.

Notice that my left hand leads the way through. The open stance provides the space, but make sure your shoulders, arms and knees are parallel to the target line.

I'm following through down the line, led by my left direction hand.

FOLLOW-THROUGH: JIM FURYK

When my stroke is off, I can usually trace the problem to one of two sources. My putter is either going inside on the back-stroke or inside in this follow-through position. I want the putter going straight back and straight through.

Bruce Fleisher, an outstanding putter, says he never looks up until he hears the sound of the ball going into the hole. I don't do that, but my head remains still even at this stage of my follow-through.

The triangle remains connected at follow-through. The reason I'm not considered a pure pendulum putter, even though my movements are similar, is the stroke path. My stroke goes straight back and straight through instead of slightly inside for the back and forward strokes.

My wrist angles have changed slightly since impact. I'm a feel putter who doesn't delegate a role for each hand. I think my hands both do a little bit of everything—direction, power and feel.

The blade continues out and slightly up as I follow through. The blade remained low on the backstroke and downstroke. It comes up slightly following impact, to apply topspin.

My putter is following a straight path at follow-through and the ball is tracking on the target line. I want a nice fluid motion through the ball.

Positioning the ball farther forward in my stance allows the putter to go through and accelerate smoothly.

My posture has remained the same, but now my head is turning up. That's OK at this stage of the stroke because my ball is farther down the target line.

JIM SUGGESTS:

You will notice the difference in speed and breaks on fast greens more than on slow greens.

On slow greens the ball doesn't break as much and won't move as much from one direction to the other. On fast greens the ball will break more the slower it goes.

Once you have confidence in your stroke mechanics, we will work with you on the main things all pros think about the most—pace and speed.

Straight back and straight through. My putting sequence was shot on the famous island green on the Stadium Course at the Tournament Players Club at Sawgrass, the par-3 17th. We play THE PLAYERS Championship there.

FOLLOW-THROUGH: ROCCO MEDIATE

This is the part of the swing I never try to control. Long putters are not meant to be swung short except for tap-ins. Once again, it's a feel thing, and the length of the follow-through happens naturally.

One tip to increase your feel is to grip your putter softly. Any time you grip a golf club tightly, you are tensing up your muscles and not allowing them to feel the shot. The putter is one club you don't want to strangle with your grip.

This is the first time a triangle has been used to illustrate my connected stroke. Just like the other pros in this book, I move in a connected and unified manner.

When you practice, visualize the bottom point of the triangle going back and through. Think of a metronome ticking your perfect rhythm.

ROCCO SUGGESTS:

For many amateurs their first putt from a long distance is a lag. I practice 30- and 40-foot lag putts. From that distance I want to get within a three-foot circle around the hole. This is a good practice drill for you.

From this distance in a tournament, if I get within three feet I'm skipping to the hole!

As the stroke plane goes slightly back to the inside, the putter head rises in my follow-through.

The long putter pendulum swing has my ball rolling along the target line. I know some people try a short pop stroke with a long putter, but I don't suggest that because it isn't as effective as the pendulum stroke.

The keys to using a long putter are:

• Keeping the butt of the grip on your sternum.

• Using your left hand to keep the grip's butt in place.

• Gripping the club with the right hand in the same manner as a conventional length putter.

• Never moving the club with the right hand.

• Using your left shoulder to take the club back and the right shoulder to move the club through.

By now, I think you understand how important it is to set up at address with a posture that is comfortable to maintain throughout the entire stroke. All of us need good posture and legs of granite. This goes for every putter type—long putters, conventional length putters, cross-handed and conventional grip putters.

As I follow through, the putter head is returning to the inside of the target line. Instead of controlling it, I'm allowing the club to swing on its natural swing path.

"Left shoulder up, ball in the cup! Left shoulder around, ball above ground!"

That is one of my favorite sayings and it certainly describes the need for correct shoulder motion. For your putter to move along a stroke plane, your shoulders must also move in a plane. Here are some drills to help develop that feeling.

SHOULDER MOTION DRILL

If you pull putts to the left, turning your left shoulder around instead of keeping it up has been your problem. This drill encourages your shoulders to move in a plane that will keep the ball on line.

You need the same dowel and bungie cord we used in an earlier drill, along with two long sticks. I've used some old shafts I put together with tape.

SETUP

Place the two shafts in the ground about one step apart (1). The shafts should be at the same angle. The dowel is across my upper arms and secured with the bungie cord around my back (2). The dowel should be touching the front of the shafts (3).

Once you set up properly, stroke back (4) and then through (5), keeping the dowel on the shafts. This provides very good feel for the arc you want the club to move on. If you performed the drill correctly, you stayed in touch with the shafts but did not bang or lose contact with them. Notice that the left shoulder finished up, so the ball will be in the cup!

SAM SNEAD VISUALIZATION DRILL

Sam Snead said a golfer should think of sliding his shoulder up the flagstick, to avoid pulling short putts.

Elements
of the
Stroke:
Follow-
Through

3 CORRECTING PROBLEMS

"The ball has to stop some-where. It might just as well be in the bottom of the hole."—Lee Trevino

Ever wish you had a PGA TOUR professional around to keep your game perfect-ly tuned? Now you have four! In the previous section you watched and analyzed their strokes. Now the spotlight shifts to you as they begin the process of improving your putting.

During their weekly pro-ams our TOUR experts see just about every putting mistake that can be made. In this chapter, Partners Club member David Rush demonstrates some common mistakes and mis-conceptions, and then the pros step in to help.

Starting with the grip and ending with the follow-through, our pros cover some major trouble areas. You will likely find some of your problems featured, and that's just fine. Everyone wants to improve their game. So take advantage. The best instructors in the world are on hand to help. After all, they sink putts for a living.

"It's amazing how putting affects your entire game. During each round you are going to face a number of five-and six-foot putts. If you can hole these putts with regularity—even if the rest of your game is average that day—you will save your score."—Rocco Mediate

PROBLEM #1

GRIP

PGA TOUR Partners Club member David Rush, from Orlando, Florida, plays to a 12 handicap. With a busy schedule and loads of traveling, he still finds time for a weekend round. He's a much better putter than he demonstrates here, but he graciously volunteered to show what you may be doing incorrectly.

David demonstrates two grips that wreak havoc with putting strokes. In both cases the palms are not facing each other, making it difficult for the hands to work together. Use a mirror at home to check your grip.

RIGHT HAND ON TOP

David's right hand is shifted too far to the front of the grip. If this resembles your grip, you have a tendency to pull the putt left because the right hand prematurely closes the blade through impact.

RIGHT HAND UNDERNEATH

Have you heard the tip about laying the grip in your open hands? Well, this is the wrong approach. The usual result of this grip is an offline stroke to the right because it creates an open clubface relative to the target line.

LEE'S GRIP

How I grip the putter in my right hand makes all the difference in the world for me. There is this certain sense of feel I need between my thumb and first finger. Once that is achieved, it's very hard for me to miss a putt. Here's how I grip my club.

PUTTER GRIP

A good grip begins with selecting a comfortable grip style to put on your putter. I prefer one that is fairly wide so I can place both thumbs flatly on top of the putter.

This feels good to me. I can hold the putter better by putting pressure on the grip with my thumbs.

RIGHT HAND FIRST

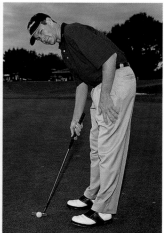

Here's one of my secrets to lining up correctly: I take my grip at the same time I'm lining my body to the target line. I place only my right hand on the putter first.

Holding the club with my right hand makes it easier to turn my head and look at the hole. If the left hand grips the club too early, my shoulder restricts the view. Accuracy requires always having a clear view of the target line as you set up.

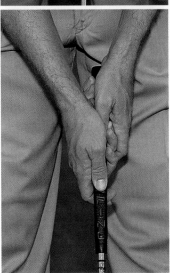

The right hand grips the club first. Notice how the thumb flatly rests on the front of the grip. I putt best when my hands mirror each other. As my left hand goes on the club, the palms face each other with both thumbs on top of the grip. This mirror image allows my hands to work in unison. That's opposite of the grips David demonstrated. Think of your putter as a delicate instrument. Your hands are the contact for your brain. Hands that work together are transmitters for feel.

DAVE'S GRIP

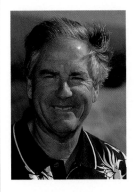

Some of my amateur partners drive me nuts as I watch them grip their putters. They set their hands on the grip and then wrap their right hand around as David Rush demonstrated. Players who yank their hands around under pressure aren't going to consistently repeat their grip.

The best way to describe how I grip the putter is that I put my thumbs on the grip first and then let the rest of my hands go on.

THUMBS ON TOP

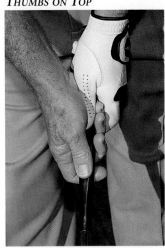

Just like Lee, I prefer a paddle-type grip with flat areas to place your palms on. Your palms should face one another. I set both thumbs on the putter first and then place the rest of my hands around the grip. The facing palms stay square to the target line.

FOURTH FINGER OVERLAP

My left index finger overlaps the fourth finger of my right hand instead of placing it in the groove formed by the pinkie and fourth finger. This keeps my hands close together.

Note: My grip pressure is not extremely tight. In fact, sometimes I have to remind myself to hold the putter a little tighter.

NINE FINGERS ON THE GRIP

My overlapping grip places all the fingers on the club except my left index finger. I place that finger in the groove formed by the fourth finger and pinkie.

My grip pressure is like holding a bird. I don't want it to get away, but I don't want to kill it either. My feel points are my right hand's thumb and second finger.

The key to my putting is the overlapping finger of my left hand. When I take the putter back, it's being taken back with this overlapping finger, which helps me keep the blade square on the way back.

Correcting
Problems

JIM'S GRIP

My cross-handed grip is how a left-handed golfer would normally putt. Lee and Dave use a more conventional right-handed grip that places the right hand lowest on the club. In my case, my left hand is the lower hand. But since I want both hands close together, it's only marginally lower.

CROSS-HANDED GRIP COMPARISON

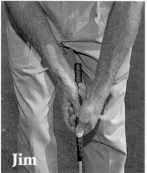
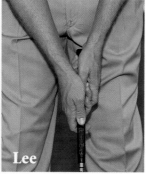

Jim

Lee

Notice how Lee's right hand is lower on his grip while my left hand is the lower one. Many teachers agree that cross-handed grips resist the temptation for the wrists to break down during the stroke.

GRIPPING THE CLUB

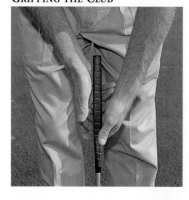

I want my hands close together on the grip. When the grip closes, the palms will be facing and the thumbs are on the front of the grip. I change putters and grips often to get a different feel in my hands.

INDEX TO INDEX

This is the third variation you've seen in the overlapping grip. I overlap my right index finger over the left hand so that it rests on that hand's index finger. I do this all in the spirit of keeping my hands as close together as possible.

ROCCO'S GRIP

I promise you won't see another version of the overlapping grip with my long putter. Because my hands are more than a foot apart! The sternum comes into play, with my grip.

GRIP INTO STERNUM—LEFT HAND

If you're doing a crossword puzzle and are looking for a seven-letter word for breastbone, sternum is the answer. It's the bone I place the butt of the long putter against. My left hand goes over the shaft to anchor the position.

RIGHT HAND GRIP

To demonstrate the ideal position for the right (lower) hand, I'm gripping my long putter with a conventional length grip. Notice the right hand grips the club so my palm is square to the target line, just as it should be with the conventional grip. I don't hold it with a claw or closed fist grip.

NO OVERLAP

Since I don't have a hand nearby to overlap, my right index finger does not close around the club. My thumb rests on top of the shaft.

PROBLEM #2

POSTURE

David demonstrates two examples of improper posture. In both cases the hands can't be positioned properly to keep the club on the correct stroke plane.

POOR HAND POSITIONS

In these sets of photos, David's posture forced his hands up (left) and then stretched them out (right). Both are actual examples of postures that came about from misunderstanding a tip. Lee Janzen comes to the rescue.

LEE SHOWS THE REASON FOR A WRISTY STROKE

Dave is standing so tall in one set of photos, Rocco needs to loan him *his* putter. In the bent position, with the arms up, I'll demonstrate the wristy stroke that results. From what I've observed over the years, the higher the hands the more likely you are to hinge and break down on the way through.

HANDS TOO HIGH = WRISTY STROKE

Standing too tall creates a wristy stroke. You'll miss the hole every time.

LEE'S CURE—ARMS HANG DOWN

I believe the more you allow your arms to hang down, the less wrist action there is likely to be. I use a short 32-inch putter that allows my arms to hang down and still grip the putter correctly.

HANG ARMS FOR PERFECT POSTURE

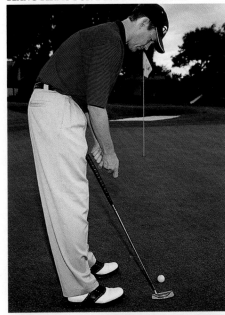

When I say reach down, I don't mean to grip the putter lower on the shaft. I reach down by slightly bending at the waist, allowing my arms to hang naturally.

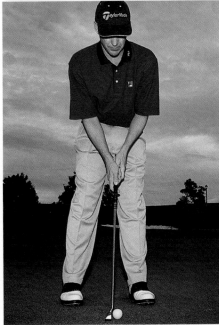

As my arms hang, notice how they match up with my putter grip. That is the reason I use a shorter putter. I've maintained excellent posture while still managing to reach down.

BALL POSITION

David demonstrates both ends of the spectrum for ball placement. One is too far back and the other too far forward.

THE PROS' BALL POSITION

Most successful putters try to be as precise as possible with their grip, address, alignment and ball position. Consistently repeating these elements leads to sinking more putts. Three of our pros demonstrate their ball positions.

TOO FAR BACK

JIM FURYK'S BALL POSITION

I like to see my ball about one-third of the way back in my stance. My stroke path goes back low and away from the ball instead of to the inside. With the ball any farther back in my stance, I can't get my putter square at impact to start the ball on the target line. For me, ball position is a timing issue.

ROCCO MEDIATE'S BALL POSITION

With my long putter's pendulum stroke, the ideal position is just off my left heel. This is the position where the club-head returns square to the target line. Farther back or farther forward would cause the face to be slightly open or closed at impact.

TOO FAR FORWARD

DAVE STOCKTON'S BALL POSITION

The width of my stance changes, based on the type of putt I have and its speed. I may place my feet a few inches to over a foot apart. Regardless of the width of my stance, my ball position is two to three inches inside the left foot.

PROPER WEIGHTING

Unlike a full swing, a good putting stroke doesn't allow a shifting of weight. How you balance yourself at address contributes to maintaining a steady lower body.

David Rush demonstrates two fairly common but incorrect weight positions. Check yourself in a mirror to see if you have this problem.

WEIGHT BACK FROM TARGET

WEIGHT LEANING TOWARD TARGET

DAVE STOCKTON'S LEGS OF GRANITE

I place 60 percent of my weight on my left foot and keep it there during the stroke. The lower body does not move during my stroke. To help maintain this position, I turn in my left toe slightly. The result: legs of granite throughout the stroke.

Problem #5:

Alignment

Do you want to consistently impact the ball square to your target line? Then make sure you are always correctly aligned. Even the pros work on alignment during practice sessions; this ensures that alignment is second nature when it really counts during a tournament.

Here David Rush demonstrates two alignment versions guaranteed to provide poor results.

Lee Janzen's Shoulders

As seen from above, Lee's shoulders and knees are parallel to his target line. This is the same position he will return to at impact without having to make any compensations.

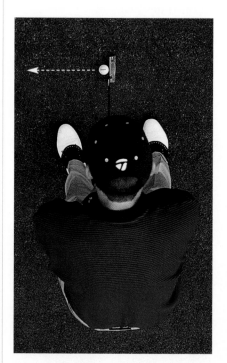

If you think a pro's game looks effortless, the reason is the lack of compensations he makes to get back to the ball. Something as simple as consistently aligning yourself correctly eliminates extra motions that negatively affect your stoke plane.

OPEN ALIGNMENT   ### *FEET CLOSED/SHOULDERS OPEN*

It's OK to have your feet slightly open to the target line, as you learned in Chapter 2, but in this case David's shoulders, arms and knees are not parallel to his target line either. His left foot is too far off line. The putter virtually has no chance of starting and returning along the correct stroke plane.

Jim and Rocco align their feet slightly closed. The major difference between their alignment and David's is seen in the shoulders. Their shoulders are parallel to the target line while David's are pointed away from the line. He made an effort to keep them from following the feet but he overcompensated.

DAVE STOCKTON'S ALIGNMENT

Dave Stockton slightly brings his left foot back from the target line to provide room for his left arm to go through toward the target. Compare this with David Rush's very open stance.

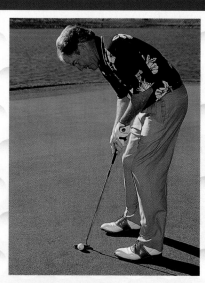

JIM'S THREE STEPS TO PERFECT ALIGNMENT

You don't need special training aids to develop an on-line target alignment. I'm using the flagstick and my putter. You can work on this at home by placing a broom parallel to your simulated target line, then follow my three steps.

STEP #1: PARALLEL SHOULDERS

The flagstick is the visual reference for aligning parallel to the target line. Hold the club across your shoulders, checking to see that they are aligned parallel to the reference line. Regardless of your foot position, your shoulders must remain parallel to this line.

STEP #2: PARALLEL HIPS

Hold your putter across your hips. The hip line should match the shoulder line. Both must be parallel to the target line.

STEP #3: FOOT ALIGNMENT

Confident that your shoulders and hips are parallel, your foot line can now be adjusted. I prefer a slightly closed stance, so I move my right foot back from the line. If you prefer an open stance like Dave Stockton, move your left foot back from the line. The key is to keep your shoulders and hips still parallel to the target line, not your new foot line.

Correcting Problems

PROBLEM #6
WRISTS

Wrist flipping may be great for flipping pancakes in a skillet. But as you putt, retain your angles, keeping your wrists firm through impact. David Rush demonstrates the ever-tempting but incorrect wristy motion (left, below). Jim's photos are alongside David's to help you develop the mental image of how to correct the problem.

WRONG: WRISTY

RIGHT: TRIANGLE BACK

Compare the wrist angles of David's wristy stroke with Jim's unified triangle backstroke. David's wrists are flipping the club back while Jim strokes back with his shoulders, arms and hands. David's clubhead is way off the ground while Jim's skims back. Jim's simple one-piece motion will keep him on his preferred swing plane while David is in for trouble when he tries to retrace his steps.

WRONG: WRISTY

RIGHT: TRIANGLE THROUGH

Wristy back leads to wristy through. David's wrists flipped through while Jim stroked through the ball. David's wrists reversed their angles while Jim retained his same angles through impact. David's clubhead is way up in the air while Jim's only came slightly off the ground to impart topspin on the ball.

PROBLEM #7
BACKSTROKE

Not properly understanding tips from friends or magazines led to the two backstroke problems David demonstrates. In both cases, his putter position is not going to allow a consistently squared impact position. If you think about taking the club straight back on line or swinging it back to the inside instead of allowing the natural plane to dictate position, here are the problems you may be facing.

INCORRECT: OUTSIDE BACKSTROKE

JIM FURYK'S ON-LINE BACKSTROKE

Jim Suggests:

These close-up photos of me at address, and also reaching the back of my stroke, look far different than David's example. Look at my ball's position in relation to the hosel. The unified triangle swing is responsible for not going back too far off the line.

Even though my club does not swing inside—like most pendulum shoulder-style putters—I consistently bring the putter back to the ball so that it arrives at a 90-degree angle to the target line. In other words, square!

INCORRECT INSIDE BACKSTROKE

LEE JANZEN'S ARC

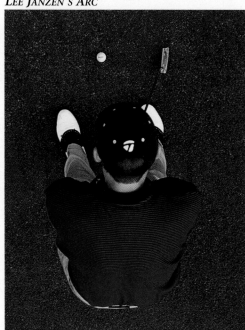

Lee Suggests:

From above, you can see my shoulders remain parallel to the target line. Notice the arc away from the ball to the inside of the target line. It's not a big rainbow or banana-shaped stroke path, but the clubhead is open, not square.

Staying connected and swinging my shoulders, arms and hands back together naturally took the club back along this stroke plane but kept me aligned. Do not swing your shoulders to the inside. Stroke the club back, allowing the arc to occur naturally.

Correcting
Problems

95

PROBLEM #8

ANGLE OF ATTACK

Do you always seem to come up short? One reason may be the angle at which your putter approaches the ball. Pros keep their putters low to the ground on the backstroke. As the action photo (right) of David Rush shows, amateur putters don't always keep the putter low. This has to do with staying on plane instead of lifting away or flipping back.

Along with direction, roll and spin suffers with a high-to-low descent to the ball. Good putters impact the ball from a level position. The clubhead rises slightly through follow-through, applying overspin on the ball. If your path is high to low, you will be applying a certain amount of backspin.

Backspin is highly desirable for lobs and short approaches but deadly for putting purposes. The backspin rotation acts as a brake when you want roll.

WRONG: STEEP ANGLE

See how David's club is making a high-to-low approach. In effect, the clubhead has negative loft. David will hit down on the ball instead of stroking through. Backspin and a shorter-than-desired ball roll will be the unfortunate result.

LEE'S LEVEL APPROACH

Notice how my putter head stays low on the backstroke. I want to be level at impact. This creates the needed topspin that keeps the ball rolling along the target line toward the hole.

LEE'S PUTTER AT IMPACT

This is the exact moment of impact. You can see how level the putter is to the ball. As the putter comes up through the follow-through position, topspin is applied to the ball, keeping it rolling on track.

PROBLEM #9

FOLLOW-THROUGH

Follow-through is vital to your stroke even though the ball is already on its way to the hole. Lee Janzen's philosophy is to follow through to the hole. It ensures he will be square to the line at impact. Follow through in either of the two positions David is demonstrating and you will be putting again.

OFF-LINE FOLLOW-THROUGH—OUTSIDE AND INSIDE

In both photos David is following through with his putter face pointed away from the hole. Both balls are tracking away from the hole in the same relationship to the target line as the putter head.

LEE FOLLOWS THROUGH TO THE HOLE

I want my putter head to be square to the line at one to two inches *prior* to impact, and stay that way one to two inches *past* impact. Having the mental image of following through to the hole helps me achieve this.

Here, just past impact, the club is still square to the line as the ball rolls on the target line.

LEE STAYS ON LINE

The ball is about halfway to the hole. See how close to the line my putter head still is. At this point, it does slightly go to the inside, but not much.

My thought is to follow through to the hole. On breaking putts you follow through to the line on which you want your ball to start.

4 DEVELOPING PUTTING ACCURACY

"The secret to becoming a good putter is simple: putt like when you were a kid. Kids don't clog up their minds thinking about putting mechanics. They just putt to make it!"—Brad Faxon

Can putting really be that simple? If it is, why do so many of us struggle with this phase of our game? As we get older, simple thoughts change into complex analysis. The mind becomes an attic filled with discarded swing thoughts and theories.

The only putting concern TOUR professionals have, after they find their line, is speed. They trust their mechanics and let all thoughts turn to making the putt.

This chapter deals with putting accuracy. Our four PGA TOUR pros show you how they select a putter and read a green, then offer loads of other information pertaining to putting accuracy.

Confidence takes over once you have a putter matched to your technique, can consistently read the correct line, and possess the needed skills to stroke your putter on plane.

"Putting affects your entire game."—Lee Janzen

IN THIS SECTION

CHOOSING YOUR PERFECT PUTTER

- Grips

- Putter head weight

- Face balanced

- Toe weighted

- Heel weighted

- Putter head loft

- Putter lie

- Selecting putters

10 TIPS TO FIND THE LINE

- How water flows

- What the cup tells you about grain

- Narrow your field of vision

- Find your dominant eye

- Plumb bobbing

- Get low

- Find the target line

- Select an interim target (2 versions)

- Develop a mental image

CONSISTENT ACCURACY

- Pre-putt routines

- Use the ball's aiming graphics

- Checklist for success

- Align to the line, not the hole

- Positive thoughts

GROOVING A TOUR STROKE

- The TOUR stroke

- Shaft is the key

- Training muscle memory

- Quicker rolling

- Martin Hall on the Practice Green

CHOOSING YOUR PERFECT PUTTER

Gary Player once responded to a question about how important his putter was. He said: "It's a marriage. If I had to choose between my wife and my putter— I'd miss her!"

He was kidding, of course, but "marrying" the perfect putter to your technique is just as important as any other putting element. You need a putter that works *with* you instead of against you. Loft, lie, aiming graphics and clubhead balance are just some of the elements that factor into your choice.

Buying the hot new putter on the market will not guarantee improvement unless it also matches your needs. If it's toe or heel weighted, for example, and you prefer keeping the club close to the line going back, the putter will fight you. You bought a club that wants to swing open and closed. So we'll start by showing how the pros make their choices.

DAVE STOCKTON

Before I show you my putters, here's a quick word about grips. I can't believe anyone who is serious about putting would choose any grip other than a paddle type. These four-sided, flat-sided grips ensure your hands fit on the club so your palms face each other. If you plan on starting the ball on the target line, put a paddle-style grip on your current putter or on any new one you buy.

PADDLE GRIPS

The first prerequisite for choosing a putter is the grip. Dave prefers a paddle style with four flat sides.

ACCURACY GRIP

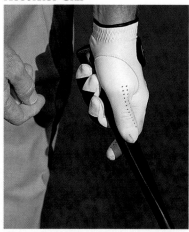

Paddle-style grips allow your palms to face each other and your thumbs to rest on the front. Dave's left hand is on the club. When his right hand goes on, he can be confident the palms will face because of the awaiting flat side.

Dave's Putters

I have two putters—a Ray Cook model that I won my two PGA Championships with, and an Odyssey. I want to see the face when I aim, so the Cook has been sanded down and is now very smooth. The top has a different texture so that when I forward press, I can see where the face is even.

Look for a putter that has an insert of a different color. This makes it easy to see when you're lining up the putt. The other important factor is putter head loft.

TWO PUTTERS

The Odyssey is more of a blade while the Cook is mallet shaped. I forward press my hands while taking the club back, so I need a putter with a lot of clubface loft. The Cook has 5.5 degrees of loft and the Odyssey 5 degrees. One may be old while the other new, but they both do the same for me because of the loft. The shaft length for each is 34 inches, but 35 inches is still within my requirements.

I added weight tape to the back of the Cook because it's light. Fine-tuning is very important, and tweaks the putter's performance to your own unique requirements.

ROCCO MEDIATE

My Scotty Cameron long putter features a sterling silver insert (see photo above). It's a very soft material that increases my feel. The other modification is shaft length.

If you want to convert to using a long putter, measure the shaft to where it will be positioned. I want my shaft to rest on my sternum when I'm slightly bent at address.

Forty-eight inches is my correct shaft length. If you are shorter or taller, have your shaft adjusted accordingly. For accuracy, adjust your shaft length instead of compromising your address position. Get a shaft length that meets your needs!

HOW IT LOOKS

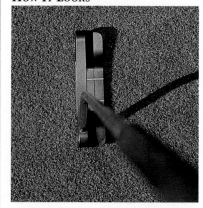

As you set up, your eyes will be inside the target line. The inclined shaft does not go vertically up and down. My pendulum stroke takes it back slightly inside, squares at impact before returning slightly inside to follow-through.

JIM FURYK

I grew up in the age of high-tech equipment. Most putters looked like the Ping Anser with the shaft in the center. I feel comfortable with different putters, but I chose the Acushnet Bulls Eye as my example. It's the best feeling putter I've ever had.

The Bulls Eye gives me good feedback. If I'm facing a 30-footer, it makes me feel I can hit the putt 30 feet. Sometimes a putter looks good but feels terrible and it's hard to judge the distances. A lot of that has to do with the shaft.

The older shafts may be better than the new ones. In fact, Tom Kite and Lanny Wadkins both claim older shafts feel a lot better. Perhaps the new materials have trouble duplicating this feel.

I have to confess that even though I've loved this old Bulls Eye for 10 years, I never used it in a tournament until the 2000 season. My putting game was struggling, and after switching to it, I finished fourth and third in my next two events. It's going to stay around for awhile.

JIM'S BULLS EYE

The clubface is toe weighted because the shaft enters very close to the center of the clubhead. My stroke stays close to the line going back and through, and the toe weighting resists the face from swinging open on the way back and resists closing on the way through. My loft specifications are either 2.5 or 3 degrees. A 35-inch shaft works the best for me.

LEE JANZEN

As you can see in the photo at right, my putter length is shorter than normal because I believe gripping with my arms hanging down reduces wristy strokes. Consequently, my shaft is 32 inches instead of the conventional 35 inches. It looks even shorter in the photo.

My putters also differ in clubhead loft. Most putters have 3 degrees of loft, but I prefer 4 to 5 degrees, with 4.5 being perfect. A caution about bending the putter to increase the loft. When you bend a putter, it may add additional loft along with an undesirable side effect: the tendency to hook the putt. This makes it harder to keep your putter square during the stroke.

If your technique is similar to mine, my suggestion is to find a putter that is milled with 4.5 degrees of loft instead of buying one with less loft and then bending it to bring it up to your specifications.

IN ACTION

My putter is toe weighted, but I also add some weighted tape in the center section. Never be afraid to experiment and try different things on your quest to get the feeling just right.

CLUBHEAD WEIGHTING

How a clubhead is weighted can affect your stroke. Ben Crenshaw opens and closes his putter through the stroke and prefers a heel weighted putter. Jim Furyk wants his club to resist opening and closing, so his choice puts more weight in the toe.

Many manufacturers produce putters that offer equal face balance. You will learn how this is accomplished in Chapter 9, but the main advantage for amateurs is that off-center hits will stay on line.

The choice is yours and the only way to determine the best clubhead weighting for your technique is to sample all types and compare the results. Do you think any of our professionals

would put a putter into play they had not evaluated? Here are some important considerations during your evaluation program:

1 Was the putter head square at impact?

2 Did the ball start on your target line?

3 Were you able to roll the ball the necessary distance?

4 Did you sense any special feeling being transmitted by the putter?

DETERMINING PUTTER HEAD BALANCE

You can quickly determine how a putter head is weighted by balancing the shaft on your index finger. Adjust the shaft until it's horizontal. The putter head visually shows the weighting. Here are some examples:

TOE WEIGHTED

HEEL WEIGHTED

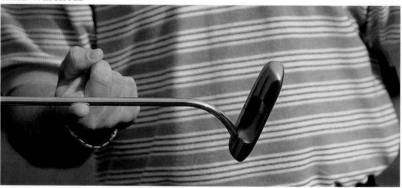

The heel points down.

FACE BALANCED

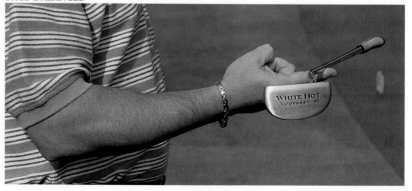

The toe points down.

The face points up and there is no evidence of weight preference for the heel or toe.

PUTTER LIE

Putters have loft and lie. Loft is the angle of the clubface and lie is the shaft angle. If you prefer standing farther away from the ball, you need a flatter lie than someone preferring to be more upright does.

You don't have to run out and buy a new putter to change your lie. Most pro shops or local club builders can adjust your lies.

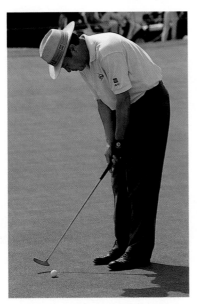

SENIOR PGA TOUR player Isao Aoki creates a flatter shaft lie by keeping his hands close to his body and putting with the toe in the air.

COMPARE THE LIES

When you choose a putter, select one whose lie works best for you. Some are more upright and some are flatter. The choice is yours.

FIND YOUR PREFERRED LIE

Using the Mitchell Fitting System, a club technician can place a gauge on your shaft and ask you to position the putter the way it feels best. The gauge shows the lie you want.

ADJUSTING THE LIE

Using the Mitchell machine, the technician will precisely bend the shaft to your exact specifications. Most cities have club repair businesses listed in the Yellow Pages.

Developing
Putting
Accuracy:
Choosing
Your
Perfect
Putter

105

USING YOUR PUTTER HEAD BALANCE

When facing breaking or uphill or downhill putts, some players prefer to position the ball on either the heel or toe of the clubface. If this is your technique, you should look for a face-balanced putter.

If you position the ball on the toe or heel (1) for certain putts, try a face-balanced putter. This model features peripheral weighting for toe (2) and heel (3) hits.

HOW THE PROS SELECT THEIR PUTTERS

Pros often try out putters early during the tournament week when the manufacturers' representatives set up by the practice putting green. Their bags rim the green and are filled with putters of different shapes and weighting. Some putters offer some high-tech innovations.

Visit a PGA TOUR or SENIOR PGA TOUR event during the practice rounds and you'll have a chance to find out what really is new in putters. Representatives generally are happy to answer questions from the crowd about some of their new innovations.

10 TIPS TO FIND THE LINE

"**R**eading the line" is an absolutely essential element of putting.

Our TOUR experts use the 10 quick tips covered in this chapter to find the line to the hole. In the next chapter you'll walk alongside them and learn what else they incorporate into their accuracy-producing, pre-shot routines.

Once you've read both chapters, your knowledge for reading the line will soar. But not your score. That should shrink.

#1
FOLLOW THE WATER

I've learned over the years to start reading the green as I walk up to it. Jackie Burke taught me a great tip to visualize the direction my ball is going to move as it rolls. If you toss a pail of water around the hole, in which direction will the water go? There is no such thing as a truly flat putt, because the green has to be sloped to allow the water to run off. The ball will always go in the direction of the water!

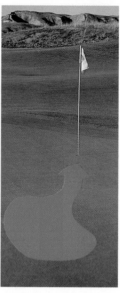

Very few putts are straight. To better read the green, visualize how the water tossed from an imaginary pail would flow.

#2
LOOK AT THE CUP

Check the direction the grass is growing. In the Northern states this is not always a factor, but in the Southern states, Bermuda is what you find on most greens.

If you live in the North but travel South to play, ask the course pro for additional suggestions in determining the grain on his or her course. Remember these tips:

• Bermuda grass greens grow in the direction of the setting sun.

• On steep portions of the green, Bermuda grows in the direction the water flows.

• Checking the cup will tell you the direction of the grain at the hole.

CHECK THE GRAIN

Grain

The smooth side of the cup is with the grain. If this side of the cup is toward you, the putt will be faster. The rough side of the cup is against the grain. If this side of the cup is toward you, the putt will be slower.

#3
NARROW YOUR FIELD OF VISION

Once you have the green's overall topography in your mind, it's time to concentrate on your line. Narrow your field of vision by placing your hands on your forehead to block out extraneous lines of sight. Too much information is hard for the brain to process; so focus in on what matters.

#4
FIND YOUR DOMINANT EYE

To become a better putter, you need to find the eye that dominates your sight. Some players line this eye up over the ball. Jim Furyk demonstrates plumb bobbing on page 110, and you need to know your dominant eye to utilize this topography-reading technique. Partners Club member David Rush demonstrates the simple procedure.

Make a circle using your thumb and fore-finger.

Hold the circle in front of you, positioning a distant object in the center of the circle. Both eyes should be open.

Not Dominant   **Dominant Eye**

Without moving the circle or your head, look through the circle with one eye open and one eye closed. Then reverse the open and closed eye. Your dominant eye is the one that allowed you to see the distant object still centered in the open circle.

Developing
Putting
Accuracy:
10 Tips
to Find
the Line

109

PLUMB BOBBING WITH JIM FURYK

GET LOW

Plumb bobbing is one way to determine which way a putt will break. It's like dropping a weight and holding the end of the attached string. You will be able to roughly determine the lay of the land and where the ball is going to break. I also use plumb bobbing to find an interim target along the target line.

- From a crouched position behind the ball, allow the clubhead weight to hang down naturally.

- Using your dominant eye, line up the shaft with the hole.

- My dominant eye is my left, and I look at the right side of the shaft to pick up the slope.

THIS IS WHAT YOU WILL SEE

The putt will break from right to left.

When trying to read a putt from behind the ball, always crouch down and get low. If the ball is close to the edge with a bunker behind it, it's permissible to get in the bunker for a low view. Just remember to rake the bunker as a courtesy to others.

Standing tall does not allow you to pick up the slight nuances of the changing terrain. The closer the ball gets to the hole, even the slightest break will send it off line. You need to plan and select a proper target line.

JIM SAYS:

The clubhead weighting helps your particular technique to stay on plane, but can hurt when trying to plumb bob. Depending on its balance characteristics, the head will want to rotate in a certain direction.

I fooled around with this technique for a long time and my results show it was worth the effort. Initially use plumb bobbing to confirm the break you already found, and select an interim target along the line. Soon you will be able to incorporate any needed adjustments while developing the confidence to consistently depend on this valuable technique.

#7
WALK TO THE BREAK

It's as simple as it gets: Just walk the green for a moment, to really "feel" the slope and gradient, and get insight into how the ball will break. Here, I've found the highest point of the target arc.

My caddie and I sometimes find ourselves saying to each other: "Wow, can you believe the ball is breaking that much?" Yes, even at our pro level, we sometimes do not read enough break into a putt. To get the feel for the main breaking point, walk the line and find the spot you feel the putt will break toward the hole. This is the highest point of the target arc for a breaking putt. The next tip shows you how to line up to that spot instead of the hole.

#8
JIM'S INTERIM TARGET

When reading a putt, I choose an interim target along the ball path. Never align yourself to the hole for breaking putts. In this photo, I've aligned myself to an interim target and my concentration is all on speed.

The X is the interim target I'm lining up to. It represents something I found on the line I want this breaking putt to start out on. It may be a discoloration or something notice- able. Don't align for or shoot for the hole on breaking putts.

Developing
Putting
Accuracy:
10 Tips
to Find
the Line

111

#9 DAVE'S CLOSE-UP INTERIM TARGET

My interim target is less than an inch in front of my ball on the target line. It's easy to line up to this interim target. After my last look at the hole, I return to look only at this interim target, not the ball. I want to see the ball roll over it.

Stroke Happens Here → ← Dave's Interim Target

My putter head is touching my interim target. I will return the club to the other side of the ball to start and complete my stroke, but this precise interim target spot is what I'll focus on.

#10 DEVELOP A MENTAL IMAGE

Don't visualize just a sunk putt. "Watch" the ball pop out and come right back to you!

The greatest golfer of the 20th century, Jack Nicklaus, has a special way to visualize the correct line for his putts. Once he reads the line, he sees the ball going down the line and in the hole. But then he sees it coming out of the hole and rolling back to its original position. Talk about target lock on!

CONSISTENT ACCURACY
PRE-PUTT ROUTINES

How much confidence would you have in a bridge that changed its support foundation for each crossing vehicle? Not much! The bridge to consistent putting success also requires a firm support structure.

Pre-shot routines provide the structural support for putting. TOUR players follow a mental checklist from the moment they walk on to the green. This organized and structured effort eliminates overlooking even the slightest detail. Even under pressure, their pre-shot routines promote confidence through familiarity with a procedural friend. With each item checked off, confidence builds, allowing full concentration for making the putt.

Routines involve marking the ball, reading the green, feeling the speed and setting up consistently. Most amateur players rarely follow a consistent pre-shot procedure, and the results show.

Join our four TOUR experts as they reveal their pre-putt routines. Glean as much as you can, and incorporate some of the ideas into your game.

DAVE STOCKTON
PRE-PUTT ROUTINE

1 When a putt has an obvious break, I line up the putt by looking at it from the low side of the hole. This one will break right to left about six inches, so I'm standing in the direction it will break. I never circle the hole, because each view would look radically different and might contradict your initial read. You are better to have a positive thought, even if it's wrong, rather than confuse yourself and be uncertain.

2 Crouching down low behind the ball helps me visualize the "highway to the hole." I see which part of the hole the ball will enter. The front door may really be on the side.

3 I'm coming up to the ball while keeping my eye on the target.

5 Still looking at the target, with my putter in front of the ball, I widen my stance by moving my left foot toward the target but slightly back from the line I will start the ball on.

6 My eyes go back to the ball with the putter head still in front. My interim target is going to be a spot less than an inch in front of the ball on the target line.

7 As I lift the club back over the ball, I take one last look at the target.

4 My right foot is placed where I think its final position will be and then I place my left foot even with the ball. I'm still looking at my target. Notice my putter is in front of the ball. The reason: When I lift it back over the ball, I use my fingers, which reinforces feel. I think golfers often make the mistake of setting themselves up parallel to the target line, take their practice strokes, and then step in. Doing that would cause me to lose sight of my target and what I needed to do.

8 This time my eyes return to the spot in front of the ball, not the ball itself. It will be rolling over that spot, on target to the hole the next time I see it.

9 You already know that my swing begins with a forward press as I simultaneously take the club back. The putt's speed will affect the target line, and we'll focus on that subject in Chapter 5.

JIM FURYK
PRE-PUTT ROUTINE

1 *I begin my pre-shot routine differently than most TOUR players. They like to read their putt, take practice strokes, and then move into the ball. Here's how I start:*

- *I take my practice strokes first. This helps me get an idea for how hard I want to hit the ball.*

- *How fast or slow the putt is will be factored into my read. For a fast putt I feel may get away from me, I will have to trickle the ball and play for more break. Uphill putts that are slow require firm hits, and that speed affects the break too.*

2 *Crouching down behind the hole makes it easier to get a more accurate read of the line. I demonstrated plumb bobbing for you earlier, and I'm using that method here to roughly determine my line and to find an interim target along the way.*

Plumb bobbing is not an exact science, but it does help. This putt will break left to right.

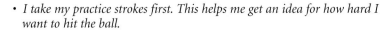
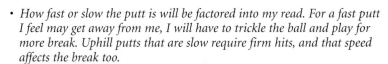

3 *I use the seam stamp on my ball as an alignment aid. Mine says Tour Professional 90. For the past few years, I just wanted to see the white of the ball, but when I was struggling with my setup, I decided to use the printing. The printing is positioned toward the general area I'm aiming, giving me something to square up to. It also helps me start the ball on the correct line.*

4 *A holed putt is the result of properly going through my pre-shot routine.*

LEE JANZEN
PRE-PUTT ROUTINE

1 The moment my approach shot lands and rolls is when I start reading the green. Roll direction provides a good indicator of how the water will drain off the green, something the architects must consider during construction.

2 Lining up your putter with the hole and the ball gives you another preliminary indication if you're going to have an uphill or downhill putt. This one is definitely downhill.

3 Always mark your ball for the two reasons I'll show you next. Place a coin or marker directly behind it before removing the ball.

4 During a tournament, my caddie cleans the ball after I remove it, but I clean it myself when playing with friends. Dirt in the dimples can send the ball off the target line.

5 Look closely at the Taylor Made line on my ball. This is the second reason for marking it. While replacing it in the same spot, I'm pointing the lettering in the direction I want the ball to travel. I do this for each putt.

6 I walk alongside my putting line toward the hole. On unfamiliar courses you can feel the subtle terrain changes and whether the putt is uphill or downhill. The firmness or softness of the green can also be felt, playing an important role for determining the speed. Some designers are masters at disguising whether a putt is uphill or downhill, using the illusion created by the putting grade against an existing hill. This can make it confusing unless you walk the line and feel the actual terrain as you adjust your balance.

7 If you take the pin out of the hole, always do it on the high side to avoid interfering with any of your partners' lies. I always use my putter to lower the flag softly onto the surface. Letting the pin drop could damage the green for a later group's putts. All golfers need to take care of the course.

8 I placed the balls in this photo by the side of the hole for demonstration purposes. Looking at the putt from below the hole, I know this putt will be breaking left to right. If I aimed directly at the hole, the ball would break and miss the hole to the right by about three ball widths. To compensate, I'll begin by aiming three balls to the left.

9 With the line firmly in mind, all my thoughts turn to speed, which we cover in Chapter 5. I take one last look to find an interim target on the line for aiming purposes. Remember my target line is going to be toward the outside ball, not the hole.

10 I'm pointing to my interim target, a discoloration along the line. My preference is to find something five feet from the ball. This gives me a better chance of making 25- to 30-foot putts because a closer target is more reliable to aim toward.

11 As I make my practice strokes, all my thoughts are on the speed of the putt.

12 Part of my pre-shot routine is how I hold the putter with only my right hand as I step into the shot. It helps me see the target line better as I align myself. In this photo, you see a confident golfer, secure in the knowledge of having done everything possible to set up for accuracy, thanks to my pre-shot routine.

Developing Putting Accuracy: Consistent Accuracy

ROCCO MEDIATE
PRE-PUTT ROUTINE

1 *I've learned over the years to check out the terrain while walking toward the green. My tip in the last chapter showed you how to visualize the direction water would run around the hole. As I'm walking up to the green, I'm doing just that.*

2 *After walking up and marking my ball and replacing it, it's time to read the putt. It's easier to read a putt farther from the ball than closer because you can see more. I get back as far as I can, unless there is something behind me like a lake or bunker. I'll get down in a bunker, but not a lake.*

3 *If I'm confident I really saw the line from behind the ball, I may not walk to the other side to read it. My usual rule for reading putts is:*

- *On downhill putts, I can see more from below the hole.*

- *On uphill putts, I can see more from behind the ball.*

I sometimes read the putt from both directions, but often you find yourself going through the motions, which doesn't always do a lot of good. Find what works best for you. Maximize the things that help you get the best read and eliminate the others.

4 *My practice strokes help determine the length of my stroke. Unlike Lee and Jim, I do not use any ball graphics to line up my putt. I prefer to look only at the white of the ball. I go by feel. Do I have an interim target? Sometimes, but not always. If you can find a discoloration or ball mark on the line, it can be helpful.*

5 *As I address the ball and prepare to initiate the stroke, I'm confident that I gave myself every chance to make the putt.*

GROOVING A TOUR STROKE

Muscles have memories, and yours are programmed for the way you putt now. The time has come to begin re-training them for accuracy, using the tips our four TOUR professionals demonstrate.

Lee Janzen begins with some overhead views to re-program your mind with simple but effective stroke thoughts. He'll have you thinking about your shaft instead of the putter head and ball.

Guerin Rife, developer of the respected Leadbetter Putting System with David Leadbetter, provides helpful ideas and methods to re-train your muscles for accuracy. He also demonstrates how to get your ball rolling quicker.

Dave Stockton reveals the "back of the hand" drill he mentioned in the Elements of the Stroke chapters. Finally, Martin Hall shows you some drills to help groove your stroke on the practice green.

A COMPLETE STROKE

LEE JANZEN

My putting stroke and yours should be a mini-version of our full golf swings. Just as the full swing follows a plane, so does the putting stroke, but to a lesser extent. If the shaft were vertical, the plane would be straight back and straight through. But my shaft and yours are angled.

This angle creates a slight swing arc. As you stroke the ball, the putter will go back a little to the inside, square up as it approaches the ball and through impact, and then return slightly inside on the follow-through. This happens naturally, once you allow the movement to begin with your shoulders and carry through into your arms and hands. Let's look at my stroke from above.

2-BACK OF THE STROKE

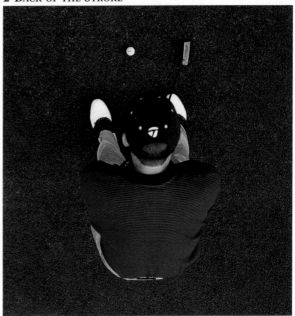

My clubhead is slightly open and slightly inside the target line. This occurs naturally, if the shoulders provide the movement and the arms and hands remain together as a unit. Remember, limited movement equals accurate, consistent stroke planes.

1-ADDRESS

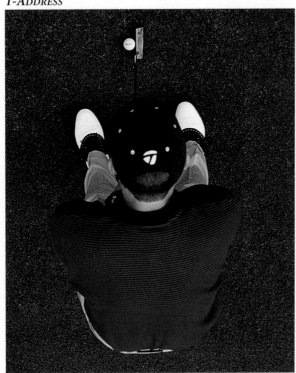

My shoulders, waist and feet are parallel to the target line. The clubhead is square to the line.

3-PRE-IMPACT

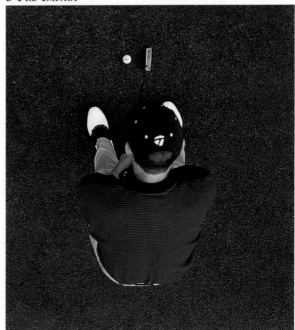

My clubhead is reaching the square-up zone. It is the zone where my putter forms a 90-degree angle with the target line. This is two to three inches prior to impact.

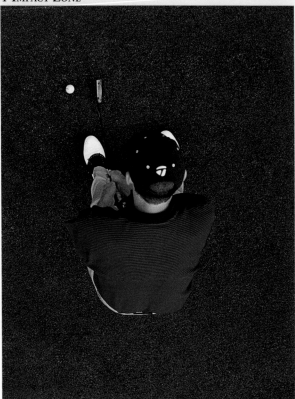

This composite action photo shows how still my head and lower body remain during the entire stroke. My shoulders provide the motion, and the arms, hands and shaft stay connected together.

My clubhead is square to the target line and the ball will start rolling on the line I selected. The clubhead will remain square two to three inches past impact.

5-FOLLOW-THROUGH

The ball rolls accurately on the target line. I have followed through toward the target. The putter head returned slightly to the inside following impact.

Notice how the clubhead arcs slightly to the inside on the backstroke and follow-through. I'm not trying to make this happen by guiding the clubhead. The angled shaft, and staying connected, creates this simple, natural and accurate stroke plane.

Developing
Putting
Accuracy:
Grooving a
TOUR
Stroke

ACCURATE BALL TRACKING

For Lee Janzen, the clubhead comes from a slightly inside position to square to the target line before impact, and then returns slightly inside to follow-through. The square zone is about six inches—three inches prior to impact and three inches past impact.

The only spin on the ball is topspin. The squared position eliminates sidespin that would move it off the target line. Notice how the putter is level at impact and rises as follow-through is completed and moves toward the target. This creates overspin—or rolling spin—to keep the ball committed to the line.

THE KEY IS YOUR SHAFT

Improvement will come quickly if you begin thinking about the shaft instead of the direction your putter head is going. Concentrating on just the clubhead and ball programs your brain to control the clubhead's direction; this is something you can't do consistently.

Once you start thinking only about shaft movement—your brain understands the shoulders, arms and hands move the shaft—a new thought process begins, complete with muscle memory training.

Are you still puzzled why the clubhead goes inside on the backstroke and follow-through? Perhaps the demonstration on page 123—with another club guiding the shaft—can better illustrate the slanted stroke axis.

SHAFT ON SHAFT
LEE JANZEN

I've set up parallel to the target line with a slight difference: I'm holding my 5-iron parallel to the line and resting my putter shaft on it. As I stroke the ball keeping the shafts together, you'll see the inclined arc naturally occur.

1-ADDRESS

As we begin, my putter head starts out square to the target line. I'm holding my 5-iron parallel to this line as the putter's shaft is placed on it.

2-BACK OF STROKE

As I continue to hold the 5-iron shaft parallel to the target line, I slide my putter back. See how the head followed a slightly inside arc as it moved away from the ball. The inclined slant of the putter shaft naturally causes this to occur.

3-IMPACT

Notice the head has returned to a square-to-the-line position at impact, the same position as we had at address. A square impact will start your ball tracking accurately like mine.

4-FOLLOW-THROUGH

Even though my 5-iron shaft still remains parallel to the target line, my putter has returned to an inside-the-line position as I slide one shaft on the other to follow through. The linkage between your shoulders, arms, hands and putter shaft makes what I just demonstrated happen naturally.

TOUR players' strokes are smooth looking because we move only the essential parts. Natural movement is far more accurate and consistent then steered movement.

Developing Putting Accuracy: Grooving a TOUR Stroke

TRAINING MUSCLE MEMORY

Now it's time to start training your muscle memory, just as Lee Janzen suggested changing your focus from the putter head to the shaft. Guerin Rife worked with David Leadbetter in developing the Leadbetter Putting System training aids.

Guerin Rife.

Rife's "12 & In" training device is unique because it develops muscle memory in the same way Lee Janzen's 5-iron demonstrated. Another important feature is that unlike other training aids, the "12 & In" lets you wean yourself off it as part of every training session.

"The finish position is the most consistent element I see in every good putting stroke," said Guerin, when asked what he noticed most while watching pros putt. "Pros hang the finish, they don't rebound. This means they come to a nice halt on follow-through with the club just hanging there instead of quickly stopping and having the club come back. They have no tension in their forearms, and you see this nice comfortable stroke. The overall impression is that it appears natural and not forced."

We also talked to Guerin about where he thinks the putter should be at follow-through.

"David Leadbetter did a lot of research when we developed his Leadbetter Putting System," Guerin replied. "He found that 90 percent of the TOUR players' strokes go slightly to the inside on the backstroke, square slightly at and after impact for about 9 inches, and finish slightly inside. It is definitely not straight back and straight through, as some other teachers advocate."

It was obvious that Guerin was talking mostly about the shaft. We asked him why.

"To re-train your muscle memory for a consistent putting stroke, you want to get away from putter head awareness," he explained. "Golf is tough enough, so it makes sense to simplify your putting stroke so it can serve you under pressure situations. Once you are able to simplify the stroke into the fewest number of moving parts—and in the case of putting it's really just a one-piece motion of your shoulders, arms, hands and the shaft—accuracy and consistency are enhanced."

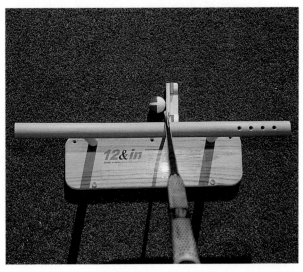

"12 & In" training aid.

Guerin went on to describe his "12 & In" Training Aid.

"It's really just a very simple training device that by guiding the shaft instead of the putter head allows the golfer to feel the natural putting stroke and repeat it over and over again," he described. "Consistency leads to confidence. Confidence is the key to putting! Once you set up the training device parallel to your target line, you rest your putter shaft on the specially designed curved rail to begin. Sliding the shaft along the rail allows you to feel and develop the same professional type stroke I described earlier. The hands and arms will be moving as one."

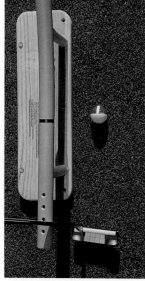

The "12 & In" is set up parallel to a target line of a 12-foot, straight putt. It's set up 12 feet from the hole because you need to feel comfortable from this distance if you want to improve your score. Good approach shots and birdie potential are statistically viable within 12 feet. The shaft rests on the rail and the putter head is square to the target line.

Sliding the shaft back along the rail brings the putter head slightly inside the target line, guided by the hands and arms in a one-piece motion. Notice the face opens slightly.

As the putter returns to the ball it squares up to the target line 3 inches before impact. The ball is marked to show how it travels along the target line to the hole.

4-IMPACT

5-FOLLOW-THROUGH

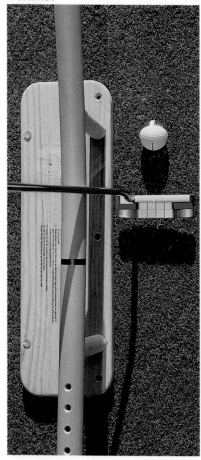

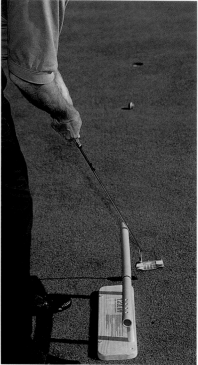

The putter head is square to the target line at impact and the ball begins its roll on the target line.

Following impact, the rail curves upward and directs the shaft, which is on an angle, to in turn direct the putter head along the target line for 6 inches. This "square zone" is created with the one-piece motion of the hands and arms.

To achieve muscle memory, make 10 practice strokes without a ball. You'll begin to feel comfortable with the movement generated by the shoulders down into your forearms and hands. Use a ball for another 10 strokes. Wean yourself away from this training aid by moving it back a quarter of an inch, allowing your natural motion and muscle memory to take over.

Developing
Putting
Accuracy:
Grooving a
TOUR
Stroke

ROLL SPIN

Golf balls are made to fly, not roll. The dimples and grass blades fit and cause friction, which slows the ball's roll. Every putt has two forces working against it: grain and gravity. The object is to get the best roll possible, with backspin being the enemy. Topspin, overspin, roll spin all mean the same thing: The ball comes off the putter face and rolls better.

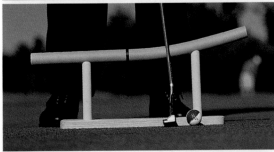

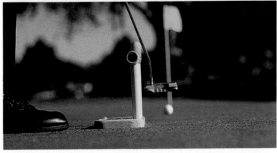

Pros apply topspin, or roll spin, on the ball. This enables it to track along the target path to the hole. Notice here how the putter, staying on the stroke plane, impacts the ball level and then rises up. Roll spin is the result.

GETTING A QUICKER ROLL

Guerin Rife recommends putters that feature grooves cut into the face. Putters normally have smooth metal faces or polymer inserts.

The grooves grip the ball, carrying it slightly up and off the putting surface before it falls off the putter face into an immediate roll. While most putters have at least three degrees of clubhead loft, Guerin's roll-groove putters have no loft, and together with the closely positioned grooves, the ball spends only a fractional amount of time on the clubface. The ball begins rolling immediately on the target line instead of skidding along the surface.

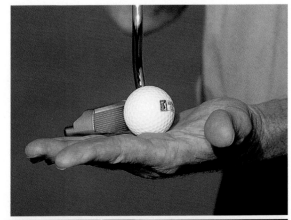

Roll-groove putters improve accuracy by starting ball roll quicker.

DAVE STOCKTON'S LEFT-HAND-TO-THE-TARGET DRILL

My left hand is my direction hand and leads the way through the stroke. My father used to hold up a club touching the back emblem on my glove. Then he would move the club out and down the line about three inches. He wanted me to lead through the stroke with my left hand so it could hit that same spot.

The average golfer will go through impact and come up with the emblem above the club. My wrist will go down and through, creating topspin.

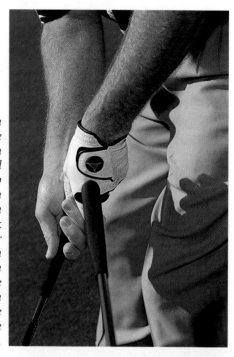

As you address the ball, have a friend hold up a club and touch the emblem on the back of your glove. Then have him back the club up on the line about three inches.

My interim target is just in front of the ball on the target line. It's a brownish piece of grass. I want my left hand to stroke over this spot.

Practice by stroking your left hand over the spot on the ground and hitting the emblem with the club. Ideally, you want to go lower, as I have. This trains your muscle memory to have the back of the left hand go toward your target past impact, ensuring the clubface will be square.

PRACTICE GREEN

If you hope to make the same consistent stroke, you must re-train your muscle memory. Otherwise, before you know it, you will slip back into your comfortable old habits. Practice these drills at home, and when you get to the course your muscles will be properly programmed.

HANGMAN'S NOOSE

This drill makes sure you don't lengthen or shorten your arms during the stroke. Keeping the string taut keeps everything at a constant distance.

Tie a knot in a rope and place the loop over your neck. Hold the string taut by holding it in your grip. This is the constant distance that needs to be maintained.

Bad **Good**

Good **Bad**

Try to keep the string the same length on your backstroke. Raising your arms or flipping your wrists will incorrectly shorten the swing. You will also feel a tug on your neck if you try to lower your arms.

Keeping the shaft in line with the string keeps the constant distance intact. If you get wristy, you can't putt very well, and in this drill the string shortens immediately if the wrists become too active.

SOCCER BALL DRILL

Have a soccer ball lying around the house? Time to use it for some putting muscle memory training. Keeping the soccer ball in place, without causing it to wiggle around, is your goal!

Place the soccer ball or another ball of the same size between your elbows. Exert enough inward pressure to hold the ball in place. Take a few practice strokes, making sure the soccer ball does not wiggle, and then address the golf ball.

Stroke back and through again, being sure the soccer ball does not move. Allow your senses to feel the relationship of the triangle formed by your shoulders, arms and hands moving together. You are well on your way toward training your muscles to a repeatable, accurate swing plane.

PUTTING CONNECTION

When Tom Watson was at his peak during the '70s and '80s, one of the keys to his putting success was the angle of his left elbow. It never changed during his entire stroke. With this training aid (available through specialty stores) and my drill, you too will eliminate your wobbly elbows.

SETUP

Place the training aid just at your elbows. Notice the triangle forming as you bring your hands together.

THE TRIANGLE STROKES THE BALL

What did Lee Janzen tell you in this chapter? He wants the relationship of the triangle created by the shoulders, arms and hands to be the only moving parts of the stroke. As you stroke the ball, the training aid keeps the triangle linked. Feel the triangle stroking back and through. Even close your eyes as you stroke back and through, feeling the triangle move like a pendulum.

ELIMINATING WRISTY STROKES DRILLS

Too much wrist action is the scourge of most amateur players. They just flap their wrists around and can't begin to control them. Here are two drills to regain control of those independent wrists.

Left Wrist Drill

This drill provides immediate feedback if your left wrist is flipping. Set up by gripping the club lower than normal and place a golf ball between the left wrist and the shaft. If your wrist angle does not change, the ball remains in place. Lose the angle and the ball falls away.

CORRECT WRIST ANGLE

The ball remained in place. Maintaining the wrist angle applied the pressure to keep it from falling.

WRISTY MOTION

Flipping the wrist eliminated the correct angle needed to keep the ball in place. Practice until you can consistently keep the ball from falling. You are re-training your wrists not to break down during your swing. Even when under pressure, properly trained muscles respond correctly.

Right Wrist Drill

I'm using an extra long tee to train the right wrist because of the greater distance between the wrist and the club. Training the right wrist can be slightly more painful if you turn the tee the wrong way, so be sure and place the pointed end on the club.

Maintain the correct pressure on the way back and the angle remains the same: The tee stays in place. Get wristy and the tee falls out.

WRIST ANGLE MAINTAINED

Maintaining the correct right wrist angle creates pressure, which keeps the tee between my wrist and the shaft. This is a good drill to do periodically to keep your wrists well trained.

WRISTY BACKSTROKE

Even slight wrist action will change the angle and cause the tee to fall. Some TOUR players do use their wrists slightly going back, but they can control them. Eliminating unnecessary wrist action is the better choice for most mid- to high-handicap golfers.

Developing Putting Accuracy: Grooving a TOUR Stroke

5 UNDERSTANDING PACE AND SPEED

"A sick appendix is not as difficult to deal with as a five-foot putt."—Gene Sarazen

Putting mechanics are easily taught and mastered, but pace and speed are sensory perceptions. Translation: You have to develop a feel for how fast to roll the ball so it can follow your target line or arc to the hole.

More putts are missed long and short than left or right. A common phrase heard around the green is, "I didn't hit it!" But seldom do you see professionals come up short. When they miss, it's usually on the high side of the hole from where the ball breaks.

When amateurs miss, it's usually short or on the low side of the hole, indicating the putt was not rolling fast enough to stay on line. The slower a ball rolls the greater the break. A miss is a miss, right? Not in this case. When you miss high you had a chance to make the putt, but when you miss low you never gave yourself a chance.

This chapter will help you develop your feel for speed. Our experts share their thoughts while demonstrating drills they use to sharpen their feel. Martin Hall's Practice Green drills work on developing the proper tempo for your stroke. Combining good mechanics with tempo and feel is the permanent fix for improved putting.

"I was taught to never leave a putt short."—Dave Stockton

PUTTING SPEED
DAVE STOCKTON

The distance you hit a putt is more important than the line. By distance I'm referring to the correct speed the ball must travel. For example, I was taught never to leave a putt short. To attain that goal, the correct speed of my putts should have the ball finishing 16 inches past the hole when I miss.

Let's look at a 30-foot putt and work together on the speed. It's the perfect example for my "One-Third Rule." Following this rule, I see a highway to the hole with three different speed zones.

SPEED TRACK

DAVE'S ONE-THIRD RULE

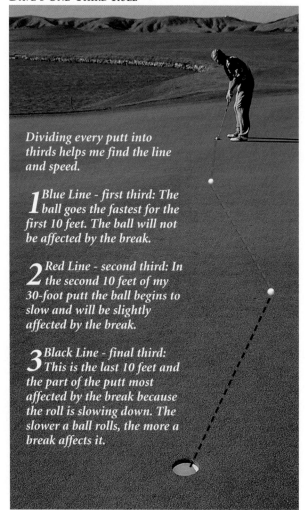

Dividing every putt into thirds helps me find the line and speed.

1 *Blue Line - first third: The ball goes the fastest for the first 10 feet. The ball will not be affected by the break.*

2 *Red Line - second third: In the second 10 feet of my 30-foot putt the ball begins to slow and will be slightly affected by the break.*

3 *Black Line - final third: This is the last 10 feet and the part of the putt most affected by the break because the roll is slowing down. The slower a ball rolls, the more a break affects it.*

I'm aligned to the target line. Speed is my only thought as I take one last look. The ball followed the target path and begins to slow as it reaches the last 10 feet. From this point gravity brings it to the hole. If I miss, the ball will roll 16 inches past the hole.

FINDING THE FRONT DOOR

It's important to understand the ball can enter the hole from any point. Breaking putts, for example, won't enter from the front of the hole. For breaking putts, the front door is really on the side.

- When you visualize your target line, see the ball entering the hole from the side not the front.

- Look at that side instead of the front as your reference point to help program your mind correctly for the distance.

In the photo above I'm placing two reference tees for this drill. From its position behind me, the ball will be breaking from right-to-left. The tee near the hole is the entrance point while the other tee is 16 inches behind the hole.

FEEL THE SPEED/SEE THE LINE

With the tees as a reference, visualize the line my ball must roll to enter on the side (left). From behind (right) can you visualize the arc it followed, taking into consideration the One-Third Rule we covered earlier? The putt broke from my right to left and the proper speed kept it above the hole until it touched the tee at the side entrance. Practice this drill to stay on the high side. To work on proper speed, use the second tee as a reference for how fast you need to roll the ball.

TWO-SIDES HOLE DRILL

Practice this drill to develop the feeling for entering the hole from different sides. To set up, place a tee an inch out and directly in front of a level hole, dividing the hole into two segments.

Use two balls for this drill. Roll one ball in on the left side and the second ball in on the right side. When you remove the tee after this drill, the hole looks bigger.

PRACTICE WITH TWO BALLS FOR FEEL

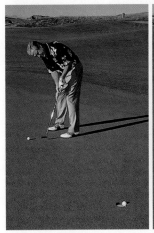

I never practice with more than two balls and typically putt within 12 feet of the hole and from various positions around it. I may start with two putts from 10 feet that break to the right and then stroke two putts from four feet that break to the left. My main goal is to constantly work on feel.

DAVE'S SPEED TIPS

- Look at your putt and determine what will make it slow down or speed up.

- Reading the green tells me the speed to hit a putt.

- Some areas of the country have their own peculiarities—in Palm Springs putts break toward Indio in the valley, and at Pebble Beach putts break toward the ocean.

JIM FURYK'S SPEED TIPS

As pros, we change courses every week, so the speed changes weekly too. We face different conditions and different grasses with different grains. How do we adjust? It's all about practice, as I'm doing at a tournament in the photo below. Practice rounds also help. Then, when the tournament begins, feeling the speed of the greens becomes natural.

Here are some of the problems I must work my way through occasionally when conditions change:

• When the greens are slower I remind myself to hit the ball.

• Going from fast to slow greens is an easier transition than going from slow to fast ones.

• The problem is feeling you will knock the ball too far past the hole, so you quit too early. The String Drill should help.

THE STRING DRILL

I even bring some training aids to my tournaments. I made this string aid myself, to help practice both straight and breaking putts.

SETUP

Twenty feet of line attached to 2 long nails or screws provides outstanding putting help. Stretch the string tight along the line you think the putt will break from. The long nails allow the putter and ball to fit under the string.

The line is set to play for eight inches of break on this putt. The key is to start the ball along this line, at the proper speed and pace. As the ball slows, it will leave the line and break into the hole.

THE STRING DRILL

My ball begins its roll on the target line (1). I aligned myself to this line, not the hole, since this is the direction the ball needs to start on. As it slows, the gravity of the break pulls the ball off the line (2). I slightly misjudged the speed and finished on the high side (3), but that's OK. Your only chance to make the putt is if the speed keeps it above the hole. My next putt (4) was at the correct speed and brings the ball into the hole from the side. Practicing with the string (5) allows me to concentrate only on the speed since the target line is visually in front of me.

DIFFERENT SPEED = DIFFERENT TARGET LINE

Speed dictates the amount of break you play. Most of the break for this putt will come in the middle. Adjust your line for the speed. Remember:

• Slower speed, play for more break.

• Faster speed, play for less break.

RULER DRILLS

All golfers experience problems occasionally. At the time this photo was taken early in a tournament week, I was correcting a follow-through problem using the rulers. My backswing was straight back, as

I want it to be, but the putter was incorrectly going to the inside following impact.

For most of the strokes seen in this book, that's OK. But I want my stroke to be straight back and straight through. Cutting across the ball added unwanted sidespin. The rulers provided reference points for keeping me on line.

JIM'S 3-6-9 DRILL

This is a drill I've used since my junior golf days. Begin by going to one side of the hole and marking off the length of your putter with tees. Doing that three times gives you distances of three, six and nine feet.

The object is to make three putts in a row from each position before moving back to the next one. Miss any putt along the way and you must start over again at three feet. Believe me, you'll be working on speed and accuracy under pressure situations. This drill works best as the last thing you do before going home, and it will build confidence as you work on your speed and accuracy.

START AT THREE FEET

Begin from three feet. You must make all three putts before moving to the six-foot putt.

IF YOU MISS

I missed my second putt from six feet, so the drill starts over again from three feet.

NINE PUTTS IN A ROW

I holed my ninth putt in a row and the third straight from nine feet. The pressure builds when you have two or three putts left to finish. You know they must be holed or you start over from three feet.

LEE JANZEN'S 20-FOOT SPEED DRILL

I never practice straight putts. Even when practicing short putts I select ones that break. Straight putts are not great indicators if you're hitting your putts solidly. But if you can make short breaking putts consistently from both sides of the hole, it shows you must be putting well.

Practicing 20-foot putts to work on speed is a drill I feel helps me develop confidence and consistency. Incorporate this drill into your putting practice session.

The key to this drill is not getting the ball into the hole, but to work on both break and speed to have it finish within the semicircle. This putt breaks about a foot from left to right so it is important to have the ball go past the hole on the left side. Passing the hole on the right side shows you didn't have enough speed to give yourself a chance to make it.

Look at the distance, visualize your target path and feel the speed needed to reach the semicircle.

- Remember that with this drill, where the ball finishes is everything. Ideally, if you miss, you should only have a short 16-inch putt coming back.

- The object is to get three putts in a row within the semicircle.

- The drill is done first in one direction and then reversed. Uphill and downhill breaking putts will help you most when working on speed.

- I putt two times in one direction and three times from the opposite side. Next, I go back to the first position for another three putts and then putt only once in the opposite direction. My goal is 10 putts in a row in the semicircle. Missing anyplace along the way means I start over.

I misjudged the speed and the ball left the line too early, finishing under the hole. This means I have to begin again.

After getting three putts in a row within the zone, now it's time to switch directions and work on a downhill right-to-left putt (1). I holed my first putt (2). That's OK, but the real goal is to get it within the zone, since making it could mean I hit the putt too hard.

I'm dialing in the speed needed to reach the semicircle (1). This is a much better effort and, as you can see, the ball is staying above the hole (2). Speed is the most important putting element to work on.

The length of my stroke is being subconsciously programmed by the feeling for the speed (3). Once again I holed the putt (4), but finishing within the zone teaches you the speed of the green. Once you can get three putts from one side, three putts from the opposite direction, three more putts from the first location and one putt from the opposite side (10 in a row) within this semicircle, you have mastered the speed of the green.

Under-
standing
Pace and
Speed

ROCCO'S SPEED DRILLS

I spend most of my practice putting working on feel. Here's a list of my normal practice drills:

1 I start off practicing five-foot putts from all sides of the hole.

2 Next, I practice from 50 feet to get the feel. I know that I'm going to have more five-footers than 50-foot putts, but sometimes a putt from 50 feet will leave you with a five-foot putt, so this practice covers all the bases.

3 I finish by sinking 50 four-foot putts in a row. It's a pain, but it really helps.

AROUND THE HOLE DRILL

From four to five feet away, drop some balls in a circle around the hole. This allows you to practice different breaks at different speeds, depending on the slope and grain.

Work your way around the hole, sinking each putt. This builds confidence for slower and faster putts with a variety of subtle breaks. As you improve, practice more severe breaks and speed changes. Then practice longer putts to develop the feel from those distances.

50 IN A ROW

My final drill of the day is to hole 50 putts in a row from around the hole.

This is not a bottomless hole. You have to pull your balls out before moving to the next location. I just sunk No. 50 and I'm done for the day.

PRACTICE GREEN

How do you presently swing your putter for long putts?

1 Long backstroke with a short follow-through?

2 Short backstroke with a long follow-through?

3 Equal-length backstroke and follow-through?

The best answer is No. 3. Matching both ends of the stroke establishes the correct tempo to start the ball rolling at the speed you feel is appropriate for the putt. We'll start with a drill to help establish equal treatment for both sides, then move on to some drills that address other important aspects of pace and speed.

TAP/TAP DRILL

This drill will help you establish a feel for equal-length backstrokes and follow-throughs.

SETUP

Place a tee where the metal shaft meets the bottom of your putter grip and another tee at the top of the grip. You need to reposition the shaft so you can place a third tee another grip length away. The outside tees should be an equal distance from the center tee.

ADDRESS

Before you address the ball place two old shafts or stakes at an angle equal to the outside tees. Place a ball in front of the center tee and address the ball.

EQUAL DISTANCE TEMPO

Stroke the putt by tapping the back shaft on your backstroke and tapping the front shaft on your follow-through. You want the sounds of the tap to be about the same. Equal sounds mean equal strokes. Another way to develop tempo is to stroke back and forth without a ball. Just listen for the gentle tap/tap rhythm.

This is a great drill to help you develop the tempo for 20-foot putts and longer.

DRIVER DRILL

You can also use the longer shaft of a driver to develop the tempo of the pendulum stroke. Choke down below the grip, keeping the shaft equidistant with the arms as you stroke the ball. Notice the shaft is resting on my sternum. Seems like we learned the same thing from Rocco Mediate for his long putter stroke.

ADDRESS

BACKSTROKE

IMPACT

FOLLOW-THROUGH

WEIGHTED TEMPO DRILL

STARTING POINT

Holding the string in my grip, I begin the drill by stroking forward. You need this initial momentum to start the weight swinging.

BACKSTROKE

Notice how the weight is staying in sync with my shaft. If I went back too quickly, the weight would be trailing my hands.

I've hung a weight at the end of a line (above), to use as my metronome to establish my stroke's tempo and rhythm. This prevents developing extra acceleration by using the hands separate from the triangle. Swung properly, with a pendulum motion, the weight will follow my putter shaft in sync.

FOLLOW-THROUGH

Matching the backstroke maintains the rhythm through the follow-through. Notice how the weight is in sync with the shaft. Smooth tempo!

WAGGLE TOES DRILL

While practicing, Nick Faldo would take his shoes off to develop a feel for proper weighting during his putting stroke. The weight ideally should be on the balls of your feet or back more toward your heels. So you should be able to waggle your toes if you are properly weighted.

WRONG

RIGHT

If you can't waggle your toes (top), your weight is too far forward.

SWEETSPOT DRILL

Two Band-Aids are all you need for this sweetspot drill. Hitting the ball with the putter's sweetspot allows the ball to roll at the speed and distance you feel appropriate. Off-center hits will adversely affect both direction and distance.

BACKSTROKE

The sweetspot is framed between the Band-Aids as the putter swings away from the ball. I want to hit the ball in the sweetspot. Staying on my stroke plane will bring the head back on plane and impact will be square to the target line.

HEAR THE CLICK

The ball was struck by the putter's sweetspot and is rolling on target. Hit the sweetspot to hear the click. Start with the Band-Aids farther apart and then narrow the gap the more precise you become.

HOLD FOR THE THREE COUNT

Holding your finish helps prevent any over-acceleration from the hands or flipping with the wrists. Once you've hit the ball, count 1-2-3. Get into the habit of holding the shaft still when you finish.

Understanding Pace and Speed

141

HOP IN THE HOLE DRILL

To do this drill correctly you need to roll your ball firmly enough so that it will climb over a shaft and go into the hole (below). The shaft will stop the ball if you hit it too softly. If you hit it too firmly, the ball will jump over the shaft and the hole.

This drill works on developing your sense of speed. It also has some side benefits.

• If you are dribbling your shorter putts just trying to get the ball to the hole, spike marks and other small undulations can knock it off line.

• This drill trains your ball roll speed. The best speed to sink your shorter putts features the ball rolling into the hole after first touching the back of the cup.

1-SETUP

Place a club shaft straight across the front of the hole. Place your putter head in the hole and line up the grip so it forms a 90-degree angle with the horizontal shaft.

2-STROKE

Address the ball with your putter head square to the target line and aimed directly at the hole. Without thinking about the shaft, feel the speed it will take to hit the ball firmly enough to have it go in after touching the back of the hole.

3-CORRECT SPEED

A ball with the correct speed will arrive at the shaft rolling straight and true.

4-HOPPING

The correct speed allows the ball to reach the shaft and hop over it.

5-INTO THE HOLE

A ball with the correct speed will go into the hole after hopping over the shaft. A ball with too little speed will be stopped by the shaft, while a ball with too much speed will jump past the hole.

THE PARKING LOT DRILL

This drill is a favorite of mine. You can do it with three clubs and seven balls before you play. Place the clubs behind the hole so they resemble a parking lot.

When you putt, you want to hit it firm enough to leave the ball a foot to 18 inches past the hole. In this drill, parked balls behind the hole are successes.

SETUP

Build a parking lot using three clubs behind the hole. Place five or more balls in a straight line (I've used seven), about a club length back from each other. I don't want to hole any putts for this drill. Rather, I want to see how many balls I can get at different positions in the parking lot, without striking each other or the clubs. Touching another ball or rail means you must start over.

MISSION ALMOST ACCOMPLISHED

MARTIN'S TIPS FOR TOUCH

• What I refer to as touch, the pros call feel.

• If you can't hit the ball with the center of the putter head, you'll never develop proper touch.

• If you have poor mechanics, you'll never develop consistent touch.

• Never work on mechanics and distance at the same time.

• Work on mechanics first.

• Work on technique the day before you play.

• Work on your touch before your round.

• I parked the first six balls successfully. Five are in the parking lot, and the sixth is just rolling in.

• In the process, I developed touch without worrying about holing the putt.

Understanding Pace and Speed

6 TERRAIN CHANGES

"Yeah, after each of my downhill putts."—*Homero Blancas, when asked if he had any uphill putts after shooting 77 in a U.S. Open Championship.*

PGA TOUR players quickly learn to handle the subtleties of terrain changes when putting on lightning fast tournament greens ... or they miss a paycheck. Most would prefer uphill over downhill putts, but pin placements, a gust of wind or the whims of the gods of golf can leave even the world's best golfers with a fast-breaking downhill putt.

Without flinching they find their line, feel the distance and go for it. They don't always make the putt, but they seldom three-putt either. This chapter reveals some thoughts and techniques our four TOUR experts use to cope with terrain changes.

Lee Janzen and Rocco Mediate demonstrate the ins and outs and ups and downs of putting, while Jim Furyk explains the "Wagon Wheel Drill." As Jim says, "This is a drill the boys in Ponte Vedra play against each other when practicing." By the way, the "Ponte Vedra boys" include the likes of Rocco, David Duval, Vijay Singh, Blaine McCallister, Frank Lickliter and Fred Funk. Not a bad collection of PGA TOUR stars.

"Your brain probably knows better than anything how much break to play. Trust it!"—*Lee Janzen*

BREAKING PUTTS

LEE JANZEN

It's the unwritten law of golf that neither amateurs nor pros play for enough break. I've seen studies that prove after we read a break we don't line up to play that break. Is it because we fear committing to a line that typically is outside the hole, especially when the putt is downhill?

Your brain probably knows better than anything else how much break to play. Trust it. The brain takes over anyway with compensations when your setup doesn't accommodate the break. The results: pushing or pulling the putt, depending on the direction it breaks.

Here are some steps to help:

- Get a feel for the speed.

- Read your putt *from the hole back*. It's important to know what the ball will do around the hole.

- Visualize the target line arc, noting where the ball will break toward the hole, and then roll the ball at the correct speed to that point where it will break.

- Set up to the line that can roll the ball to that breaking point. Don't subconsciously align to the hole.

- Think only about speed, not mechanics or the line, as you address the ball.

VISUALIZE TARGET ARC LINE

START THE BALL ON LINE TO THE BREAK POINT

I see the target arc in my mind. Notice I'm aligned to the break point, not the hole, and I'm feeling the speed the ball needs to roll to that point. Gravity, along with some remaining momentum, will feed the ball down the hill from the break point to the hole.

If you stroke the ball too fast and overshoot the break point, it will end up left and past the hole. If you stroke the ball too slow, it will undershoot the break point and likely won't reach the hole, leaving you with another tricky downhill putt.

DOWNHILL PUTTS
ROCCO MEDIATE

I'm facing a downhill putt. You seldom have a straight downhill putt, and this is a perfect example why I have to read the putt from a position that's downhill and off to the side.

Read a downhill putt from a position downhill and off to the side.

HOW WOULD YOU READ THIS BREAK?

1-READING THE PUTT

I know the general direction the ball will break. Reading the putt from below the hole, and to the side the ball will be breaking toward, lets me see the break and the hill it will be rolling down. It's important to locate the spot the ball will break. I know this putt is going to be fast, and that figures into how much break I want to play. I have this line firmly in my mind before walking to the ball.

2-PRACTICE STROKES

Once I know the line, speed is my only thought. Downhill putts have to be hit softer. Let the gravity of the green have it, don't force it. Feeling your practice strokes programs your brain for the needed speed.

3-FOLLOW-THROUGH

Even with downhill putts, always follow through. Rhythm and tempo must be maintained. Hit the ball softly but rhythmically.

4-ANOTHER HOLED PUTT

The ball rolled to the breaking point and then gravity brought it to the hole. Comparing a tournament course's green speed to your home course is misleading. You may need to hit your downhill putts a little firmer than I did to achieve the same results. Your feel for speed must be for the course you are playing that day.

UPHILL PUTTS
ROCCO MEDIATE

Uphill putts require making adjustments to your technique. Once again, feel must take over because mechanical putters are not good putters.

My backstroke may be longer for an uphill putt. My practice stroke programs the distance, and then I just let it happen. My suggestion: Try to feel the ball rolling up the hill.

Another difference between uphill and downhill putts is the amount of break. Gravity plays a role in both. Downhill putts will break more than uphill putts.

READ THE PUTT

I read uphill putts from behind the ball because you can see the hill and the break from down low. The feel for the amount of speed you'll need can be detected when looking uphill.

1-CONFIRM THE LINE

If I'm not certain of the line reading it from behind the ball, I go uphill for another look. My second read, usually to confirm what's in my mind, will be behind the cup and off to the side.

2-GO FOR IT

Visualize the ball rolling on the line you read to the hole. Always have the line and speed in your mind before committing to hit the putt. Align yourself to the point you want the ball to start rolling on, not the hole. Stroke the ball on plane for success.

LEE'S MULTIPLE BREAK TIPS

Some putts present you with the challenge of multiple breaks. Here's Lee Janzen's advice:

- For putts with multiple breaks, the last break is the most important.

- As the ball slows down it breaks more.

- Read the putt from the hole back. This putt breaks four feet from the hole (#1).

- Determine where on the severe slope the putt has to head for that point (# 2).

- The gravity of the severe slope will take care of the distance, so determine the slope break-point target and the speed needed to get it to stop there. Gravity will take it the rest of the way.

Multiple breaks are a real challenge. Read the green before diving in!

WAGON WHEEL DRILL

JIM FURYK

Some of the most recognizable names on the PGA TOUR live in Ponte Vedra, Florida, home of the Tournament Players Club at Sawgrass, site of THE PLAYERS Championship. The TPC at Sawgrass is also our practice facility when we're at home, so it's not unusual for a bunch of TOUR players to be hanging around the practice green at the end of the day.

Use this drill to practice making putts from all around the hole. Each side of the hole provides different breaks and speed, and even provides a competitive opportunity. And it's fun. Compete against your friends as you try to make 15 putts in a row from around the hole.

1-SET UP THE WHEEL

My suggestion is to place tees around the hole in the 12, 3, 6, and 9 o'clock positions. We do the drill from six feet, but you should start with three-foot putts. Start with a level putt, and then find a hole on a hill to really improve.

2-WAGON WHEEL DRILL RULES

- *You have to make all three putts from each of the four tee placements, starting at 12 o'clock.*

- *Once you make three in a row from one position, move clockwise to the next. As you move to a new position, you will gain experience putting uphill, downhill, left to right and right to left.*

- *Make three putts from the remaining positions and then three more from the 12 o'clock position so that you hole 15 putts in a row.*

- *If you miss a putt, you must drop back one clock position.*

3-MAKE THE PUTTS

You must hole three putts in a row from each of the four positions around the wheel. These are six-footers, but you should start at three feet.

4-MISSING

The rule is you have to hole three in a row from each position. I missed so I have to go back one clock position. You never have to go back past the 12 o'clock home position.

7 SPECIAL PUTTING SITUATIONS

"The ball takes a funny little bounce here or a putt takes a funny little turn there. It seems like a man ain't the master of his own destiny when he's playing golf."—Sam Snead

Webster's Dictionary defines putting as "a golf stroke made on a putting green to cause the ball to roll into or near the hole." Old Noah Webster either never played golf or always pulled out a mashie niblick to chip when he got on the fringe.

Unless you are in some pretty long grass, putting off the fringe might be a better shot to play for some golfers. Of course, sometimes a little creativity is needed. You can still putt, just not with your putter.

This chapter is about creativity with your putting stroke around the green. As Lee Janzen demonstrates, you can use your putter or a wood. Although, in his case, he prefers his rescue club.

The ever creative Rocco Mediate occasionally points only his putter's toe at the ball when it's up against the fringe, a technique used effectively by the late U.S. Open champion Payne Stewart. Rocco also demonstrates his drill for lag putting. Even pros face 30-footers on occasion. Hopefully, all your funny little "bounces" and "putts that turn" will be in the right direction.

"Even an average putt from the fringe will get you very close."—Lee Janzen

PUTTING FROM THE FRINGE

In some fringe situations, you'll want to reach for your putter and not a wedge.

With a short fringe in good condition, I may reach for my putter instead of chipping the shot. The advantage is that even an average putt from the fringe will get you very close to the hole.

With very tight grass it's difficult to chip because I want to get the club under the ball to control it. So putting becomes a viable option if the ball can be rolled through the fringe and the speed controlled.

Fringe with thicker grass makes it harder for the ball to stay on line at the proper speed. Professional golfers feel we can hole any shot from 150 yards; this includes balls on the fringe. If the highest percentage for success points toward a putt over a chip, that will be my choice. Here's how I play it.

The grain is going with me, making it easier to putt. If the grain was growing toward the ball, the resistance would quickly take the ball off line. If the photo above looks familiar, it should. It's my normal address position. My putter head is square to the line along with my shoulders and hips. My feet are slightly open and the ball position is just slightly back from normal (inset photo).

My normal putting stroke brings the putter head back square to the ball (top). The ball will roll along the top of the fringe grass (above) and up toward the hole once it reaches the green. Hit it solid to get the ball rolling. For this to be a high percentage shot, the grass has to be short and growing away from the ball. If the grass is longer or growing toward me, I still have other options, but I'll need another club for that job.

The ball reaches the green and will roll to the hole.

Special
Putting
Situations

RESCUE PUTT

LEE JANZEN

From the same lie on the fringe, here's another way to play the shot. I see guys on the TOUR use 3-woods, but I prefer the versatility of my 18-degree rescue club. It has more loft than a wood and it's a little shorter, making control a lot easier. The sole (bottom of the club) is like a wood, so it serves the same purpose.

1-THE SETUP

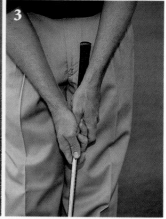

I positioned the ball off my back foot (1). My feet are together (2) and I grip down to the metal of the shaft (3) because it's a longer club than my 32-inch putter.

2-THE STROKE

My goal is to keep the ball very low and have it skim over the fringe and start rolling once it reaches the green. This requires more of a hands-dominated backswing (1) rather than a shoulder-type putting stroke. At impact (2 and 3) notice how my hands are in front of the clubhead, decreasing the loft. With 18 degrees of loft I'm not worried about closing the face down too much to get the job done. As you can see, the ball is skimming over the fringe. My follow-through (4 and 5) resembles my putting stroke. The wrist angles do not break as I follow through toward the hole.

DOWNHILL RESCUE PUTT

LEE JANZEN

Chipping the ball down from short grass above the hole is a hard shot to stop, especially on the fast greens we play every week. If I can roll the ball through the fringe instead of chipping it, this is the shot I'll play. Once again, I rely on my rescue club, but you can use a 3- or 5-wood.

THE STROKE

The ball is played well back past my right foot with my hands ahead of the clubface (1). The clubhead is lined up on the target line but my feet are together and opened to the target line. This is a very short and delicate shot. Shortening the club prevents it from stubbing the ground and bouncing into the ball.

Calling it a backstroke (2) exaggerates the small distance I take the club back. The rescue club's mass will handle just the amount of roll I need. This is better than swinging longer. Impact (3 and 4) provides just enough energy to roll the ball through the grass.

The hands lead the clubface, de-lofting it. As I follow through (5), the remaining loft of the clubface creates a slight amount of backspin braking. Then gravity takes over, bringing the ball down the slope and toward the hole.

ROCCO'S TOE HITS

Sometimes when the ball is up against the fringe, the blade of the club can get in the way. For that situation, and to amaze your friends, practice this toe shot. All good players improvise whenever the situation demands it, but having practiced the shot previously is the only way to go.

By the way, you don't need a long putter to play this shot. Payne Stewart mastered it with his conventional putter.

1-ADDRESS THE TOE

My address is the same as normal except for the putter head. The head's toe is pointing to the target line. Be sure you point the toe to the center of the ball, to avoid pool cue sidespins.

2-BACKSTROKE

DO NOT steer your putter away from the ball or back to it. Use your newly developed swing mechanics to stay on plane. The length of the stroke depends on your feel for the distance. Practice helps because the ball will pop up prior to rolling.

3-IMPACT

The putter head followed the inclined plane, then the toe impacts the ball, popping it away from the fringe. The toe cleanly got through the grass to the ball. The full face might have had difficulty making clean contact.

4-FOLLOW-THROUGH

The ball will be on the target line when it lands. The clubface stays on the stroke plane as it arcs back to the inside.

ROCCO'S LAG PUTTING TIPS

Why is lag putting in the special situations chapter? Because it deviates from the normal feeling that you can hole every putt from 30 or 40 feet. I know I can't make every one, so, realistically, any lag putt from that distance which ends up within a three- to four-foot circle will have me skipping to the hole with delight.

When I do this drill it's usually on a flat putt instead of one with undulations in the ball path. Looks like I made a few. You will too, once you realistically start thinking about getting within the circle and don't become overly concerned with sinking the ball.

I practice my lag putting from distances outside of 30 feet. A different zip code perhaps, but pros have to deal with this putt too! Don't try to go past the hole. Your goal is to be inside the three- to four-foot circle.

8 PRACTICE HAVING FUN

"Putting is like wisdom—partly a natural gift and partly the accumulation of experience."—Arnold Palmer

PGA TOUR player Len Mattiace won the inaugural Dave Pelz World Putting Championship, and credited putting practice games for his victory. Games can ease the tedium of mundane practice sessions. In other words, they make practicing fun.

Spending hours on the green is not anyone's idea of having a good time. But playing games or challenging yourself boosts your interest level.

In this chapter, two Partners Club members, Gail Flanagan and David Rush, take to the practice green with some entertaining ideas to infuse interest into your practice sessions. Gail plays Stymie with some friends, and David demonstrates games suggested by our four professionals.

"I never practice with more than two balls."—Dave Stockton

STYMIE

How do you practice precision putting under pressure? Try playing Stymie, a game two-time New York State Women's Amateur champion Gail Flanagan learned as a junior golfer. While growing up at Westchester Country Club, she attended golf schools given by then assistant professional Jim McLean. Blending tradition with competition, McLean taught them Stymie.

Stymie putting developed from the old days when you couldn't use a marker on the green. If a playing partner's ball was in your line and your putt, you would be forced to take a different route to the hole because you were blocked or stymied. Games developed as a result.

McLean instinctively knew that having 10 kids on a practice green, putting at the same hole, quickly hones their competitive instincts. They're strategizing while sharpening their skills trying to make the putt or stymie another player by leaving a ball in their way.

STYMIE RULES

When Gail Flanagan (left) visited her friend and former Arizona State University teammate Kelly Leadbetter (right) at The David Leadbetter Golf Academy at ChampionsGate in Orlando, Florida, she explained the game's rules. Mickey Novack, clubfitting consultant for the Leadbetter Academy and the 1981 PGA National Open Putting champion, joined the competition.

Stymie is best played with three or four people, but two can play if they use two balls each.

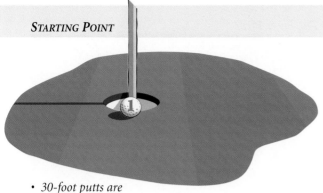

- 30-foot putts are
  the best distance to begin with.

- The first player tries to make the putt.

- If he or she misses, a "good leave" is just on the front lip. This blocks or stymies the next player's attempt to make the putt.

- Hitting another player's ball is a two-shot penalty. When only two players compete and use two balls each, hitting your own ball is a one-shot penalty.

PENALTY

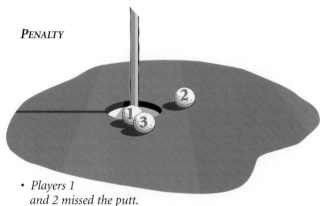

- Players 1
  and 2 missed the putt.

- Player 3 incurs a two-shot penalty by hitting Player 1's ball.

- If you hit another player's ball and cause it to go into the hole, that person is credited with a score that would be the same as if they had holed the putt.

STRATEGY AND PRECISION

- On this right-to-left putt, both players missed the hole.

- Player 2 is away and must putt first.

- Playing for the break, Player 2 has the correct speed and allows the hill to bring the ball into the side of the hole.

  - Stymie develops your feel for speed and accuracy.

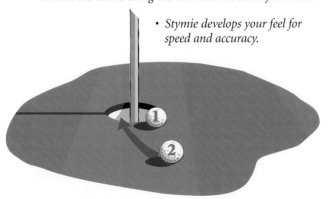

STYMIE

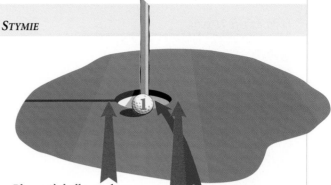

- Player 1's ball was short
  and is blocking the center of the hole.

- Player 2 incurs penalty strokes if he or she hits the ball.

- If this is a breaking putt, Player 2 can make the putt by locating Dave Stockton's open door on the side of the hole and missing Player 1's ball.

- Player 2 can also play it safe by going to either side for an easy tap-in.

TWO-PLAYER STYMIE

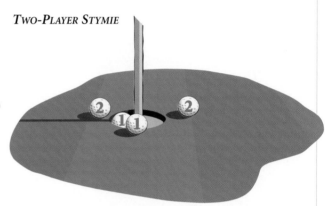

If only two players compete, each uses two balls.

SMALLER HOLE

- All three players left the putt short.

- Player 2 is away.

- Player 1's ball position effectively reduces the circumference of the hole.

- Player 2 faces the pressure of holing the putt into a smaller target without touching Player 1's ball and receiving a penalty.

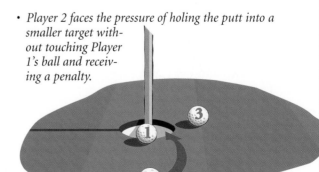

HAVING THE HONOR

Keeping honors is a big advantage. All players putt from the same starting point—in this case Gail's guitar pick ball marker.

THE FIRST PUTT

Thirty-foot putts are the best way to start, but as the game progresses and you know how the putt will break, try playing on shorter holes, concentrating on holing your putts. Kelly won the previous hole and has the honor of going first.

UNDER PRESSURE

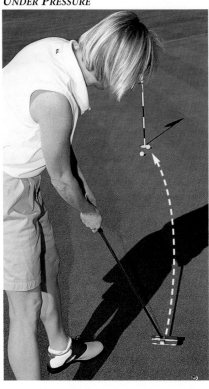

Kelly missed short and left. Only slightly blocked, Gail goes for the hole. The reduced cup size makes this a challenging putt requiring the utmost precision under pressure. She holed the putt. This photo shows her line.

STRATEGY

Mickey chooses not to risk striking Kelly's ball, and plays a safe shot to the right side of the cup. Shots like this help steel your nerves while developing a feel for the target and distance. An aggregate scoring formula keeps you in the game even if you lose a hole.

SCORING

The player with the lowest score wins. If you hole your first putt on a hole, you get zero. An aggregate scoring system is used to keep it interesting. As an example, Player 1 holes his or her first putt. Player 2 makes 3. Player 3 hits another player's ball, incurs a two-shot penalty, and makes a 5. The aggregate scoring is:

- Player 1 is 8-up. The score comes from the three shots from Player 2 and the five shots from Player 3.

- Player 2 is 3-down to Player 1 and 2-up on Player 3.

- Player 3 is 8-down.

SMALLER CUP

Golf specialty stores sell all sorts of aids to spark your interest during a practice session. This hole reducer fits inside the cup, limiting the size of the opening. The numbered zones divide the circumference into easily seen entry zones to help target different lines to the hole.

David had several target line options available for this left-to-right putt. The slower the speed, the more break he will have to play. To hole the putt, yellow is the front door he needs to enter.

Practice
Having
Fun

SCORE A GOAL

Place two tees less than a hole width in front of the hole to test your speed and accuracy. The object is to roll the ball through the goal and into the cup. Start with a flat putt before switching to a more difficult breaking one.

The tees will be in front of the hole for the flat putt. For breaking putts, feel the speed you need and then place the tees on the side of the hole the target line arc enters. Scoring goals on the practice green builds confidence as you increase your experience for feel.

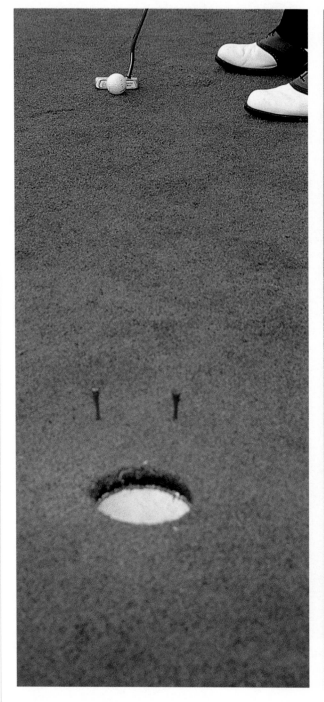

ACCURACY CHECKER

You can find all sorts of alignment aids, like this Triangulator. How accurate are you compared to your friends? Now you'll know for sure.

1-AIM

Begin by aiming to the hole.

2-SECURE THE AID

 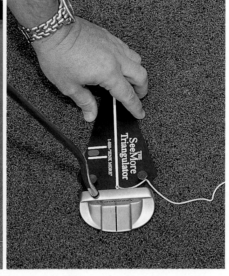

Keeping your putter in the same position, place the Triangulator firmly against the face. The aid allows you to insert tees to keep it in place.

3-AIMING RESULTS

Stretch the string out, making sure it's directly over the white line on the Triangulator. This verifies your aiming position. In this case, David was perfect.

4-SPEED TO THE FRINGE

Remember the childhood game of pitching pennies with your friends to see who could get closest to the wall? In this case, you putt to the fringe to develop a feel for the speed of the greens. Play it with your friends and win balls instead of pennies. Putting to just reach the fringe from both uphill and downhill lies takes your mind off the target, allowing you to concentrate on speed. This is also a good individual game to play before taking some pre-round practice putts. Putting with confidence grows once you develop a feel for the green's speed.

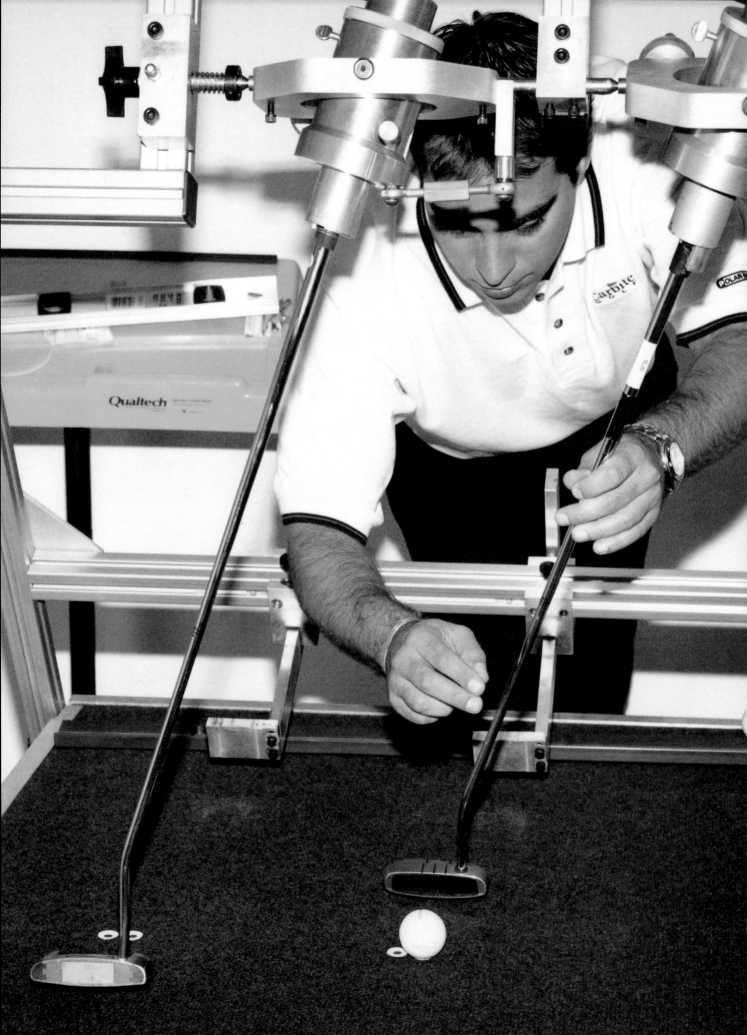

9 EQUIPMENT

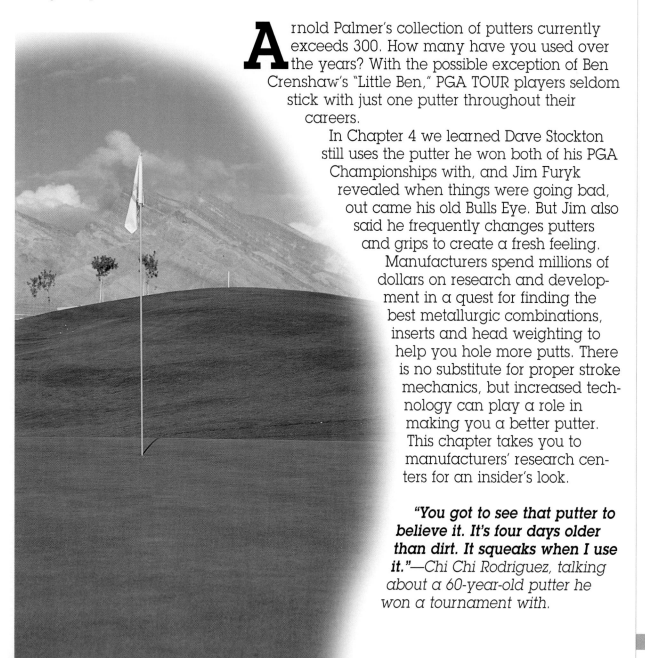

"That's a bag full of indecision!" —*Jackie Burke's comment when Arnold Palmer brought 8 putters to a tournament.*

Arnold Palmer's collection of putters currently exceeds 300. How many have you used over the years? With the possible exception of Ben Crenshaw's "Little Ben," PGA TOUR players seldom stick with just one putter throughout their careers.

In Chapter 4 we learned Dave Stockton still uses the putter he won both of his PGA Championships with, and Jim Furyk revealed when things were going bad, out came his old Bulls Eye. But Jim also said he frequently changes putters and grips to create a fresh feeling.

Manufacturers spend millions of dollars on research and development in a quest for finding the best metallurgic combinations, inserts and head weighting to help you hole more putts. There is no substitute for proper stroke mechanics, but increased technology can play a role in making you a better putter. This chapter takes you to manufacturers' research centers for an insider's look.

"You got to see that putter to believe it. It's four days older than dirt. It squeaks when I use it."—*Chi Chi Rodriguez, talking about a 60-year-old putter he won a tournament with.*

RESEARCH AND TESTING PRODUCE BETTER PUTTERS

Callaway Golf, manufacturer of the Odyssey putter, is located in Carlsbad, CA, north of San Diego. Its executive offices and several manufacturing plants are nestled close together, forming a campus-type setting fitting for a company on the cutting edge of design and technology. Research and testing are their keys to creating great putters.

DESIGN

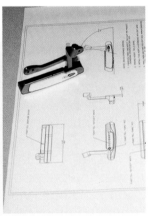

Computers are used to design Callaway's putter heads. Technical blueprints are another step in the development, testing and eventual production of the Odyssey putter you find in your local pro shop.

Putter designs begin on a computer, but the real input comes from both the Callaway testing center and its staff of PGA TOUR players. Player input is important to the company. Striving to develop more feel and reaction between the putter face and the ball, an Odyssey innovation was to have the face and the ball made of the same material. The "White Hot" line of putters was the result.

Odyssey's White Hot putters feature an insert made of the same material used in Callaway balls.

Austie Rollinson, director of product design, explains the advantages:

"Golfers need performance and also feel. One unique aspect of this material is that it provides a very soft feel along with good resilience. The problem with most other insert materials is that when you get softer with them they also get dead."

"We designed our Callaway balls for both good resilience and feel. It made sense to put the cover material in the putter head too. We tried it out with extremely positive results."

Austie Rollinson, director of product design.

QUESTIONS & ANSWERS

Q Austie, what's the average length putter Odyssey manufactures?

A The most popular length is 35 inches. It's about the longest length most players will use, including the TOUR pros. We sell other lengths, from 32 inches up, but stocking that many different lengths in a pro shop is not feasible. If golfers need shorter shafts, ask your pro to cut down the shaft to the size you specify, or special order a putter.

Q What lie angle do you incorporate into the putters? (For reference, see Chapter 4's "Choosing Your Perfect Putter" section.)

A The Odyssey lie is 70 degrees, which is slightly flatter than much of the industry. Most putter lies are 72 degrees. When Odyssey first started, we found that most professionals wanted 70 degrees. We supply putters 2 degrees more upright and 2 degrees flatter for golfers who want them. It's very tricky to adjust the lie of your current putter. If that's your choice, be sure a competent technician does the job.

Q Can you give us some information on the Odyssey putter's clubface loft?

A Our White Hot putters have 3 degrees of loft. Most other putters in the industry are 4 degrees. We found the White Hot material in our insert and the position of the center of gravity worked best at 3 degrees. Four degrees was the standard 10 to 15 years ago when the conditions of the greens were not as good as they are today. With the advent of soft spikes and modern mowing equipment, you really don't need that much loft to get the ball up on top of the putting surface.

Q What are some of the specific requests you receive from TOUR players?

A They request us to change hosel locations, change specific balance points by adding different inserts or tungsten in the sole, do a bit of grinding here and there. They are very particular in the way a putter sets up. It has to be completely square, and they may even ask for different line configurations for aiming purposes. Sometimes they even want a specific shaft frequency (shafts range from soft to firm).

Depending on the type of greens they're playing, or their technique, some pros may ask for different lofts. For example, some pros want less loft for quicker greens. We make a lot of 5- and 6-degree loft putters for the SENIOR PGA TOUR players who play on slower greens.

We call all of this "the flavor of the month." When a pro finds something he likes and it works for him, word spreads like wildfire and we get requests from other pros. That can last for a few weeks, then the process begins again. Our pro request turnaround time is a 2-day delivery for the White Hot series. Some of the designs we feature for consumers came out of this customization process, so you could say our putters are TOUR inspired.

Q What about the metal used in the head?

A We use a "303" stainless steel material. It's pretty soft, mainly for the feel and workability through our process. The last thing you want is a ding on your putter, so my suggestion is to always use a putter head cover for protection.

DAVE STOCKTON SAYS:

I always keep my putter covered and in the woods section of my bag. Your putter is the shortest club in the bag. If left unprotected and kept with the irons, it becomes easily scratched. Any marks, scratches or dents can throw you off track while aligning the club with your target line.

MANUFACTURING

Callaway's Odyssey facility strictly monitors all phases of the manufacturing process as the parts come together for final assembly. Inserts are positioned, shafts inserted and lasers are used to ensure every Odyssey putter leaves the factory with a perfectly centered grip.

◎ *ODYSSEY GOLF*

OUR MISSION.....
Establish ODYSSEY GOLF as the industry leader in product quality, customer service, and manufacturing efficiency.

The company's mission statement hangs from the rafters, ensuring quality control is always uppermost on the minds of the Odyssey personnel. Another Callaway innovation is the group stretching session the workers look forward to several times a day.

THE FINAL ASSEMBLY AREA

Equipment

GRIP POSITIONING

Austie Rollinson explains: "We spare no expense ensuring our grips are correctly positioned. It's very important because it influences several areas of the stroke, beginning with setup.

"When golfers put the face down and think it looks open or closed, it has to do with the grip and where the hands are. Off-center grips create poor aiming situations and less confident feelings."

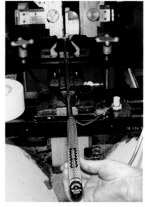

Lasers project the centerline, ensuring the perfect centering position for every Odyssey grip. Unless the grip is properly squared, your putts will be off line.

The lesson to be learned from this if you plan on having your present putter re-gripped: Make sure the technician centers the new grip properly!

TESTING

Special Projects Manager DeeDee Lasker directs Steve Hosid through a testing session in the Callaway "Confidence Room."

Aiming tendencies, ball roll and wrist angle positions are just some of the areas looked at in the testing facility. One thing that every golfer can quickly relate to is the need to have the head lie flat on the ground. That should be your initial thought when buying a new putter. If the lie angle or shaft length is not suited to your style, look for another model.

The testing also reveals putting styles along with the recommendation for clubhead weighting to complement it:

CLUBHEAD WEIGHTING CONSIDERATIONS

STROKE	WEIGHTING	SHAPE
Straight back and through strokes	Face-balanced	Mallet
Inside to square to inside	Heel or toe	Blade

Interestingly, Callaway's testing also discovered that golfers aimed mallet-shaped putters more accurately, yet prefer blade models. Factor this in when testing new putters. The rule of thumb in putter selection is choose what works best for you.

TESTING BALL ROLL

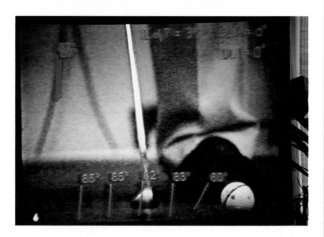

Coming off the clubface, the ball needs to start rolling as soon as possible. Skidding will sometimes veer it off line because of grass inconsistencies. Once rolling begins, the ball tracks better and will roll over those inconsistencies, staying on the target line.

Callaway's testing found better putters dynamically impact the ball at zero to negative loft. Using the wrong loft for a specific technique is revealed and then corrected, based on what is quickly seen on the screen.

Based on this testing, if you play in different parts of the country, you may want two putters:

• Less loft if you play on bentgrass greens.

• More loft if you play on Bermuda.

FINDING A PUTTER

With so many putters available on the market, how can you find the best one for you?

• Never buy a putter unless you test it against your current one.

• You already know what your putter is capable of doing, so use that as a benchmark.

• Make sure the clubhead lies flat on the ground.

• Do the aiming graphics and lines help or confuse you?

NEW TECHNOLOGY BEATS MISS-HITS

San Diego is the "Silicon Valley" for putting technology. Carbite is another innovative putter manufacturing company located in the area. Their highly successful infomercials in past years made the company famous as innovators in helping golfers consistently reach the hole even with miss-hits. Carbite putters are widely available in pro shops and specialty stores. Chet Shira is the chairman of Carbite.

QUESTION & ANSWER

Q Chet, What prompted you to develop a putter that could compensate for miss-hits?

A Several of us attended a Dave Pelz putting school and were impressed with his findings on where players with handicaps from 0 to 40 were striking the ball on the face of the putter. As the handicap goes up, that spot gets to be 2 inches wide. We realized the putters available at the time would not tolerate that type of miss-hit. Serious distance and direction errors were common as a result.

Carbite Chairman C. S. "Chet" Shira.

We felt there was a need to develop a better putter, and through our metallurgical knowledge of both very heavy and very light metals, we devised a way to design one. We place tungsten (a heavy metal) on the very ends of the putter and a lighter metal in the center to provide a resistance to twisting. This way, the higher handicap golfers can tolerate the miss-hits.

Q In theory that sounds good, but how could you test this repeatedly?

A We ran hundreds of robotic tests to verify our putter, versus any other putter on the market, would continuously give a golfer better control of the direction and distance even on miss-hit putts. Every putter makes the grade if you hit it dead center, but our putters are very tolerant of the miss-hits Pelz's research addressed.

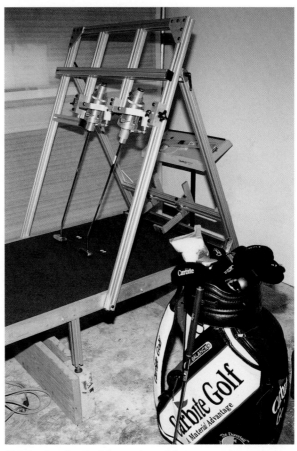

Face-balanced Carbite putters feature heavier tungsten on the periphery to resist miss-hit face twisting.

"Yipless"—the Carbite testing robot.

Q With your accomplished and distinguished metallurgy background prior to getting into putting manufacturing, has your research discovered anything about the face or insert material?

A We did find that certain putter surfaces are much more tolerant of where you hit the ball. For instance, the position of the dimples on the face. They seem to be immune to any problem and the ball will start out straight every time.

Two kinds of surfaces are most accurate:

1 High-friction putter face surfaces comprised of little hard particles.

2 Almost any of the urethane surfaces used as inserts.

Carbite uses a high-friction putter face.

Q What are the intolerant surfaces to watch out for?

A The worst are the hard, plain metal surfaces. If you have a 3-foot putt with a hard metal face and hit it on the side of a ball dimple, it will veer off a couple of inches.

Conversely, the high-friction face, common on our putters, or the very soft face features of the urethane inserts, are more tolerant of this situation and will start the ball off on your line.

Q Is there anything else that contributes to the ball going off line, even if a golfer has outstanding stroke mechanics?

A We are constantly doing research on making perfect putts. In the process, we also found there are ways of manufacturing balls better to help players play better. We are still in the R & D (research and development) phase of this, but it's become very obvious through our robotic testing that some balls currently available are not perfect rollers.

We are at the stage where we know we can do it, and we can now license the technology to the ball manufacturers. But all of this is a side benefit of our constantly active program of product testing to help golfers of all handicaps.

Q Your commitment to find the perfect putt is reminiscent of the quest to find the "Holy Grail."

A I'm an avid golfer and have been for many years. Just like anyone else, I hate missing a putt. Hopefully, my pursuit of perfect putting will help everyone who loves the game as much as I do. Putters are made out of metal, and that's my background. That makes our putters different than any other putter on the market.

Q How do you combine metals to make a better putter?

A To be honest, my first attempt was a commercial failure. Being from aerospace (Chet spent 11 years with Rocketdyne), I learned about the tremendous family of materials that were tolerant of cryogenic to ultra-high temperatures.

My first effort to make that perfect putter by positioning tungsten out on the toe and heel with titanium in the center was so expensive to manufacture that we had to sell it for $300. It was the predecessor of where we are today.

Back in the lab we substituted aluminum for titanium, but joining it to tungsten is not easy. But we found a way. It's called diffusion bonding. The metals are joined at a temperature of 1,200 to 1,500 degrees under high pressure for a short period of time. That combination allows the atoms to diffuse between the two metals.

That's how we make our Carbite putter today, with the heavier weighted tungsten as far away from the center of gravity as possible, making it resistant to twisting and sending your ball off line. We call it "face-balanced."

FACE-BALANCED TESTING

Paul Romano divides his time between the PGA TOUR and SENIOR PGA TOUR. He works with pros. Perhaps the best demonstration of all, according to Paul, is "to use the robot we developed for putting, named Yipless, proving our theory that a more perimeter-weighted putter will help golfers make more putts."

"Yipless takes all the variables out of the equation. To get a fair and valid test, we use the same putter, the same ball and the same amount of hit. This is accomplished by just letting the gravitational force of the putter hit the ball and then repeating the test using the same method."

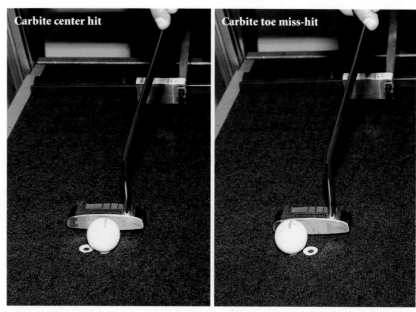

Two putters are tested—the Carbite face-balanced putter against a shaft-weighted putter. The photos above show only the Carbite putter. "Yipless" will also be adjusted to ensure that both putters' center-hit balls travel the same distance.

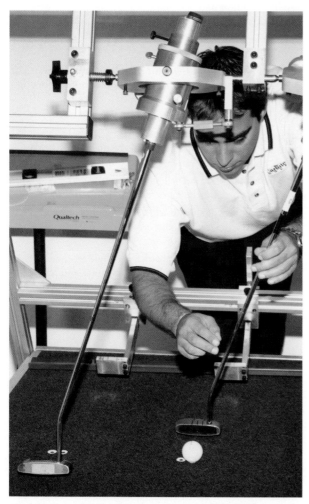

Carbite Tour Rep Paul Romano prepares "Yipless" for a test of the Carbite face-balanced putter against another putter.

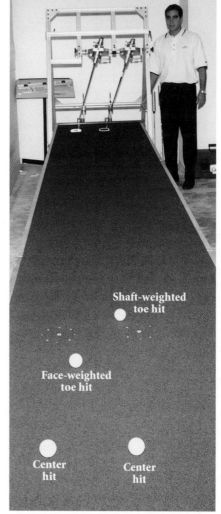

The Carbite face-balanced putter is on the left and the shaft-balanced putter is on the right. The photo at right shows the results of where center and miss-hit balls finished. The center-hit balls for each putter went through the outlined hole area, indicating similar performance. On the toe miss-hit, only the Carbite face-balanced putter was able to resist twisting and still get the ball through the outlined hole.

Equipment

GLOSSARY

Address Your body position (posture, alignment, ball position) as you set up to the ball.

Addressing the Ball Taking a stance and grounding the club (except in a hazard) before taking a swing.

Approach A shot hit to the green.

Apron Slightly higher grassy area surrounding the putting surface. Also referred to as fringe.

Away A player who is farthest from the hole. This player plays his or her ball first.

Backspin The spin of a golf ball that is the opposite direction of the ball's flight.

Ball Mark The damaged, indented area in the ground caused by the ball when it lands on the green.

Ball Marker Something small to mark the position of your ball on the putting green. You should leave a marker when you remove your ball both to clean it and also to allow your playing partners to have an unobstructed line to the hole. Markers can be purchased and can be attached to your glove. You may also use a coin or similar object.

Birdie One stroke under the designated par of the hole.

Blade To hit the ball at its center with the bottom edge of your club.

Blocked Shot Hitting a ball on a straight line to the right.

Bogey One stroke over the designated par of the hole.

Bump and Run A type of approach shot that lands and then rolls onto the green and toward the hole.

Bunker Also referred to as a sand trap.

Carry How far a ball flies in the air. If a water hazard is in front of you, you have to figure the carry to be sure you've taken enough club.

Casual Water A temporary water accumulation not intended as a hazard. Consult the published *Rules of Golf* for information on the relief you are entitled to.

Chili-Dip Hitting the ground before contacting the ball. The result: weak, popped-up shots also called "fat."

Divot Turf displaced by a player's club when making a swing. Divots must be repaired.

Double Bogey Two strokes over the designated par for a hole.

Draw A shot that curves from right to left for right-handers and the opposite for left-handed golfers.

Drop The act of returning a ball back into play. Consult *The Rules of Golf* for correct information on circumstances where this occurs.

Eagle Two strokes under the designated par for a hole.

Fade A controlled, slight left-to-right ball flight pattern. Also can be called a cut.

Fairway Closely mowed route of play between tee and green.

Fore A warning cry to any person in the way of play or who may be within the flight of your ball.

Green The putting surface.

Gross Score Total number of strokes taken to complete a designated round.

Ground the Club Touching the surface of the ground with the sole of the club at address.

Halved the Hole The phrase used to describe a hole where identical scores were made.

Handicap A deduction from a player's gross score. Handicaps for players are determined by guidelines published by the USGA.

Honor The right to tee off first, earned by scoring the lowest on the previous hole.

Hook A stroke made by a right-handed player that curves the ball to the left of the target. It's just the opposite for left-handers.

Hosel The metal part of the clubhead where the shaft is connected.

Hot A ball that comes off the clubface without backspin and will go farther than normal as a result. If a lie puts grass between the clubface and ball, the grooves can't grip the ball to develop backspin. Understanding this, a golfer knows their ball will come out "hot" and plans for that.

Lateral Hazard A hazard (usually water) that is on the side of a fairway or green. Red stakes are used to mark lateral hazards.

Lie Stationary position of the ball. It is also described as the angle of the shaft in relation to the ground when the club sole rests naturally.

Local Rules Special rules for the course that you are playing.

Loft The amount of angle built into the clubface.

Match Play A format where each hole is a separate contest. The winner is the individual or team that wins more holes than are left to play.

Mulligan A second ball that's hit from the same location. The shot that's tried again. Limited to friendly, noncompetitive rounds.

Net Score Gross score less handicap.

Par The score a golfer should make on a given hole. Determined by factoring in 2 putts plus the number of strokes needed to cover the yardage between the tee and green.

Provisional Ball A second ball hit before a player looks for his or her first ball, which may be out of bounds or lost.

Pull Shot A straight shot in which the flight of the ball is left of the target for right-handers and right of the target for left-handers.

Push Shot A straight shot in which the flight of the ball is right of the target for a right-handed golfer and left of the target for a left-hander.

Rough Areas of longer grass adjacent to the tee, fairway green or hazards.

Shank To hit a shot off the club's hosel.

Slice A stroke made across the ball, creating spin that curves the ball to the right of the intended target for right-handed golfers and to the left of the target for left-handers.

Stance Position of the feet at address.

Stroke Any forward motion of the clubhead made with an intent to strike the ball. The number of strokes taken on each hole are entered for that hole's score.

Stroke Play Competition based on the total number of strokes taken.

Target The spot or area a golfer chooses for the ball to land or roll.

Top To hit the ball above its center.

INDEX

PGA TOUR PARTNERS CLUB